HBR'S 10 MUST READS

for
Executive Teams

HBR's 10 Must Reads series is the definitive collection of ideas and best practices for aspiring and experienced leaders alike. These books offer essential reading selected from the pages of *Harvard Business Review* on topics critical to the success of every manager.

Titles include:

for
Executive
Teams

HARVARD BUSINESS REVIEW PRESS
Boston, Massachusetts

Library of Congress Cataloging-in-Publication Data

Names: Harvard Business Review Press, issuing body.
Title: HBR's 10 must reads for executive teams.
Other titles: Harvard Business Review's ten must reads for executive teams |
    HBR's 10 must reads (Series)
Description: Boston, Massachusetts : Harvard Business Review Press, [2023] |
    Series: HBR's 10 must reads | Includes index.
Identifiers: LCCN 2022060457 (print) | LCCN 2022060458 (ebook) |
    ISBN 9781647825188 (paperback) | ISBN 9781647825195 (epub)
Subjects: LCSH: Senior leadership teams. | Leadership. | Success in business.
Classification: LCC HD66.7 .H48 2023 (print) | LCC HD66.7 (ebook) |
    DDC 658.4/092—dc23/eng/20230227
LC record available at https://lccn.loc.gov/2022060457
LC ebook record available at https://lccn.loc.gov/2022060458

ISBN: 978-1-64782-518-8
eISBN: 978-1-64782-519-5

Contents

for
**Executive
Teams**

Reinventing Your Leadership Team

by Paul Leinwand, Mahadeva Matt Mani, and Blair Sheppard

AS COMPANIES STRIVE TO BUILD COMPETITIVE ADVANTAGE in a world obsessed with digitizing (which is often a must but rarely differentiating), they find that what they need from their leaders is changing. Their top people must be able to reimagine the company's place in the world and transform the organization to live up to a more ambitious purpose. That will mean fundamental change not only in the executives themselves but also in how they collectively manage and lead the firm.

Consider, for example, how the skills that leaders need for success have evolved—and the degree to which many executives are seen to struggle with these new demands. A recent survey conducted by Strategy&, PwC's global strategy consulting business, highlighted the importance of balancing certain characteristics that on the surface look paradoxical. We used to accept, for instance, that leaders could be either great visionaries or great operators. No longer. Companies now need their top people to perform both roles—to be strategic executors, in other words. They're also expected to be tech-savvy humanists, high-integrity politicians, humble heroes, globally minded localists, and traditioned innovators (see the exhibit "Six paradoxical expectations of leaders"). Not only did large majorities of the survey respondents agree on the importance of those roles, but they also voiced alarming concern about leaders' lack of

Six paradoxical expectations of leaders

In a 2021 survey of 515 businesspeople from around the world, respondents placed high importance on leaders' ability to balance the paradoxical demands inherent in six key roles. At the same time, they had much less confidence that leaders could effectively manage the tensions involved.

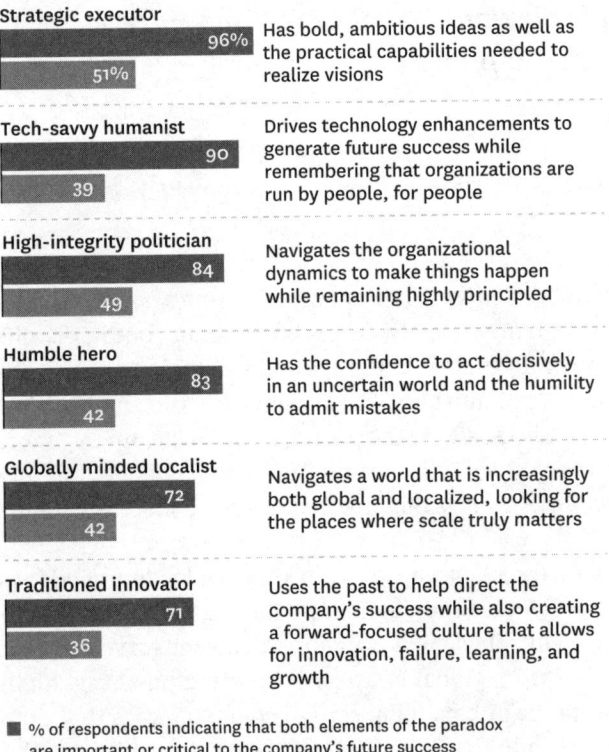

Strategic executor
96%
51%
Has bold, ambitious ideas as well as the practical capabilities needed to realize visions

Tech-savvy humanist
90
39
Drives technology enhancements to generate future success while remembering that organizations are run by people, for people

High-integrity politician
84
49
Navigates the organizational dynamics to make things happen while remaining highly principled

Humble hero
83
42
Has the confidence to act decisively in an uncertain world and the humility to admit mistakes

Globally minded localist
72
42
Navigates a world that is increasingly both global and localized, looking for the places where scale truly matters

Traditioned innovator
71
36
Uses the past to help direct the company's success while also creating a forward-focused culture that allows for innovation, failure, learning, and growth

■ % of respondents indicating that both elements of the paradox are important or critical to the company's future success

■ % of respondents indicating that top leaders in their organization are good or best in class at both elements of the paradox

Source: Strategy&.

Idea in Brief

The Problem

To thrive in our increasingly complex world, companies must move beyond digitization and reimagine what they do to create value. But most leadership teams aren't set up to transform their organizations and position them for success in the future.

The Way Forward

CEOs need to fundamentally rethink their leadership teams so that their top executives focus on advancing meaningful change rather than managing the current business.

The Steps to Follow

CEOs should identify the leadership roles needed to shape the future of the company, put the right people in those roles, emphasize the drive for transformation, and take ownership of their top team's behavior.

proficiency in them. Addressing a company's leadership gaps, however, is not merely a matter of building individual executives' skills. Although that's certainly desirable, the need to improve collective leadership is urgent.

As part of the research that led to the book *Beyond Digital,* from which this article is adapted, we interviewed senior executives at 12 prominent firms (Microsoft, Inditex, Hitachi, and nine others) and gleaned insights as to why expectations for leadership have changed. It is clear that if companies are to thrive in the years ahead, they must build new forms of advantage rather than just digitize what they are doing today. Accomplishing that means being ready to shed past belief systems and define new, bolder value propositions. Companies have to switch from competing with rivals to cooperating with partners in networks and ecosystems to create value in ways that no single organization can manage alone. Leaders need to be willing to challenge every aspect of their company: its purpose, its business model, its operating model, its people, and themselves. And conventional ideas about managing have to be inverted. Executives must move away from focusing on their individual areas of responsibility and responding to needs bubbling up from below; instead they must work together as a team to shape the organization's future and steer a path toward it.

In the following pages we draw on the experience of the companies we researched to show CEOs how to build a leadership team that is up to the challenge. This approach has four key components:

- *Identifying the leadership roles needed to transform your company for the future.* For your company to remain relevant, it will need distinct capabilities that allow it to deliver on its purpose, along with leaders who can envision its new place in the world and mobilize it to get there. What positions do you need on your executive team to make that happen?

- *Assembling the right people.* Having identified the roles your team needs, you next have to think about who will best fill them. Which individuals should you bring together so that you have the necessary talent and diversity in the C-suite to generate new ideas, challenge traditional thinking, and collaborate on meaningful change?

- *Focusing your leadership team on driving the company's transformation.* You and your colleagues will need to advance the company's agenda—and that means spending energy and time on the big priorities for the future, not just responding to the demands of the organization today. What structures and mechanisms will help you lead the company to its new destination?

- *Taking ownership of your leadership team's behavior.* Building the distinctive capabilities that will allow you to create real advantage requires a high degree of collaboration and a commitment to developing a team mentality so that the disparate parts of your organization operate as a harmonious whole. How can you build trust and a culture that powers the organization's collective success?

While we've listed these measures in sequential order, you will have to work on them simultaneously, because they reinforce one another. Don't worry about getting everything right on the first take, including how you establish the team itself. No high-performing leadership team we know was built overnight, nor did it do everything perfectly. But don't let that be an excuse for failing to make substantial progress on all four fronts.

Identify the Roles You Need

When CEOs look at the organizational capabilities their company must have to create value in the beyond-digital world, they often conclude that they have to add some nontraditional leadership positions and eliminate a few traditional ones. That has led to an explosion of new C-suite titles in recent years: chief innovation officer, chief data officer, chief sustainability officer, chief analytics officer, chief behavioral officer, chief brand officer, chief customer officer, chief design officer, and so on.

What's important, however, is not the titles but the fact that these roles focus the organization on the capabilities that are critical for delivering on your emerging value proposition. Those may involve working collaboratively with external partners. Microsoft, for example, put in place a corporate vice president for One Commercial Partner, a program to simplify its engagement with other companies that sell and support Microsoft products. The decision to create this senior role reflected the importance of the ecosystem to the company's ability to serve customers, and it ensured that partners would be represented in high-level decision-making.

The roles you choose to have on your leadership team send a message about the strategic destination you've chosen and how you are transforming to get there. Apple's creation of the chief design officer position in 2015, for example, signaled to the organization (and, in fact, the world) that design has huge importance for the company. Establishing the role greatly helped it attract the world's best designers, from the fashion industry and elsewhere, and produced one of the most differentiating capabilities that Apple has ever built.

Getting to a capabilities-based leadership model does not have to be done in one shot via a major reorganization, but leaders often regret not having moved fast enough on key positions. The more your top-team roles are aligned with the outcomes necessary for future success, the better. And if you conclude that you need, say, a chief digital officer or a chief analytics officer for a transition period, don't set up those jobs as "pirate ships" that exist outside the core structure for building and exploiting your capabilities; instead make sure you integrate them with the actual work of your company and the outcomes you seek.

Assemble Your Team Thoughtfully

Having the right roles on your top team isn't enough. You must also fill the positions with the right people—those with the skills, behaviors, and experiences you require. Thinking about the six paradoxical expectations of leaders we mentioned earlier will help. Not everyone on your team has to excel at balancing the tensions involved in each one, but collectively you should have them all covered. Where do you have gaps? Which capabilities can you develop from within the current team, and which should you bring in from outside?

It's also valuable to have leaders who can see problems and opportunities from a fresh perspective and who hold themselves—and their colleagues—accountable for tackling the most pressing and daunting challenges and realizing your aspirations. You should therefore seek people who look, think, feel, and act differently than is customary in your organization, and you should be open to—and encourage—being challenged. In fact, you might have to stop assessing new hires using the old paradigm of "How will this candidate fit in here?" and instead ask, "How will we fit with this person?" So when you look for the right talent, look beyond the usual suspects. Perhaps your next leader will be someone who once managed an unruly ninth-grade classroom, coached a sports team, or ran a local government. The people who can steer your company's future do not have to be cut from the same cloth as traditional leaders with MBAs or engineering degrees.

To be clear, we aren't suggesting running a corporate diversity initiative that makes for a colorful page in your annual report, or recruiting atypical individuals out of pure altruism or a sense of social commitment. Those motives may contribute to your thinking, but this is really about strategically building the diversity you need so that your leadership team represents the future your company is envisioning. Look for people with varied experiences, who have worked within different ecosystems and understand the capabilities, technologies, channels, and transformational approaches you will be deploying. You want leaders who have demonstrated that they can build and scale up the capabilities you aim to perfect. Your team should also reflect the diverse voices of your total ecosystem—including the customers you seek to serve, your workforce, and your partners. Very likely, those voices will cover a range of gender identities; national, racial, and ethnic origins; abilities; and economic and educational backgrounds.

Carla Kriwet, who formerly led the connected-care business at the health technology company Philips, told us that her leadership team there "sometimes [felt] like the United Nations." But she considered having such a multicultural group a necessity. As she explained, "If you have a team full of Americans who think of Europe like one U.S. state, that won't work because health care systems and reimbursement models are very different [from one country to the next]. If you only have Europeans, and they don't understand how the large hospital chains in the U.S. work and what their issues are around cybersecurity and safety, that won't work either. . . . Therefore, one of the top requirements for people to join my leadership team was that they needed to . . . actually have lived [abroad] so they know what the cultural differences mean."

Focus Your Team on Driving Transformation

One CEO we worked with spoke of feeling ineffectual until he made a fundamental shift in how he managed his work: "I used to spend all of my time responding to other people's issues through email, meetings—the entire day was making decisions related to what others provided. One day I recognized that the only way to *lead* the company was to do the work I felt was required for the organization to move forward."

Time is the top team's scarcest resource. What are the executives in the C-suite going to focus on, and how will they ensure that the urgent does not crowd out the important? Given the complexities of running a successful business today, it is more important than ever for your leadership team to be very deliberate about how it sets its agenda. It must make sure it drives transformation, rather than letting the agenda be driven by requests coming from below.

Leadership teams will always need to manage two distinct responsibilities: running the business day-to-day and building for the future that they've committed to. Philips's CEO, Frans van Houten, explains: "We talk about the need to both perform and transform. If you only transform but don't perform, you have no here and now. If you only perform but don't transform, you have no future. Therefore, in our scorecards we measure both. In our reviews we talk about both. And the targets that I give to all my executives . . . always [include] some transform objectives."

Some companies create a separate group to manage their strategic transformation effort in order to prioritize and protect it. Usually this group includes many of the executives responsible for operations—and to infuse new thinking, it may even include lower-level employees. Regardless of the governance approach you choose, make sure to hold yourself and your team accountable for addressing difficult questions about how best to shape the future.

The role of the leadership team does not stop with making big choices; senior executives must also see that their decisions are successfully implemented. That's what the "strategic executor" leadership paradox is all about. Your top people will need to get their hands dirty working through the implementation details and making sure that the activities of disparate parts of the organization add up to a coherent whole.

Howard Schultz, the former CEO of Starbucks, understood this. When he ran the company, he envisioned its coffee shops as a "third place" where people would spend time, beyond their offices and their homes. And he got involved in the nitty-gritty of bringing his vision to life—deciding, for example, that employees should grind beans to create appealing aromas rather than using flavor-locked bags of ground coffee. He also had big espresso machines replaced by smaller ones so that customers could more easily interact with the baristas making drinks. He ordered the removal of products near the cash registers, because although they generated revenue, he felt that they detracted from the experience that distinguished Starbucks from competitors such as McDonald's and Dunkin' Donuts. Schultz even helped select the music that would play in the coffee shops.

Take Ownership of Your Team's Behavior

Many companies experience a lot of rivalry in their top ranks. People may compete over who's managing the strongest P&L performance, whose function contributes most to the bottom line, or who will succeed the CEO. This individualist thinking, while rewarded in modern corporations because it sometimes drives accountability, gets in the way of transformation. Your goal should be to have everyone in the executive suite aligned around an understanding of why your company must change, what unique place in the world you're aiming for, and which differentiating capabilities you will need to get there. All your team members have to wholeheartedly own the transformation program and see their personal objectives and agendas tied to its success.

Creating ownership around the vision isn't enough. You must also create a shared purpose: Why does your team exist? What big issues is it here to solve? When defining their areas of responsibility, your people should believe that leading the company through its transformation is their most important task and that success will depend on the collaboration of team members rather than on the sum of individual units' performance. You also need to establish that when the executive team gathers, it is not to approve or reject proposals but to create value together.

Perhaps the most effective mechanism for engineering collaboration is to get pairs of leaders to work jointly on solving company-wide issues. As you reinvent for the future, you'll face no shortage of challenges, and meeting them will require the development of complex capabilities across your leadership team. Encouraging pairs of executives to join forces enables them to merge their strengths, get to know each other better, and gain a clearer understanding of the drivers of success and the constraints that exist in areas outside their own spheres of influence. When they come up with solutions, they can share the praise and see the power of bringing different perspectives to bear on big, complicated problems.

How to Tell If Your Leadership Team Is Actually Leading

WE LIKE TO CHALLENGE TOP EXECUTIVES TO THINK THROUGH whether they spend their time together really leading the company and propelling growth. Consider the following questions to judge whether you and your team make the most of your meetings.

- How much of your time is spent running the day-to-day versus shaping the future?

- How much of your time is spent reacting to what others in the organization bring to you, rather than driving the top team's agenda?

- How often do your strategic discussions lead you to make hard choices about your company's future?

- When your team spends time on strategy, do you focus on the external environment or the bold choices that your organization must make?

- How much time do you spend reviewing actions after the fact versus proactively shaping actions and a direction?

- How often do you ask people to come back with more-detailed proposals because your team doesn't quite have the energy or the clear vision to be decisive?

- How often do you spend time debating who is responsible for solving an issue rather than addressing it?

- How often do you and other members of the leadership team work together on issues?

- How well do you know your colleagues on the leadership team? Do you get the feeling that they care about your success, and do you care about theirs?

You may be surprised by the answers. Some teams find that more than half their time is spent in rather unproductive ways. Much more significantly, they realize they aren't dedicating the energy to the transformation that will position their company for success in the future.

This type of collaboration requires trust, which may be scarce among hypercompetitive senior leaders. CEOs thus need to encourage confidence that everyone is truly invested in the team and its mission. Otherwise a large-scale transformation won't work. Philips's van Houten recounts: "I started to take my executive committee to off-sites . . . in order to have the difficult discussions, but also the personal reflections. What are we here to achieve? What does success look like? But also: Why are *you* here? Do you want to be here? And if you are here, can you change your tune in how you transact with each other?"

Addressing how a team behaves is not about getting leaders to like one another and agree. It is about encouraging everyone to put issues on the table, solve problems together, come to decisions quickly, and feel committed to each person's success. That's why effective teams create rules and mechanisms for members to feel comfortable asking for help or calling out their colleagues for not following through on promised actions. At Philips, the executive committee off-sites incorporate speed-dating-style feedback exercises. Each day every member has to connect with five others and share two things: an appreciative comment about the other person and a suggestion to help that person grow in the job.

A major transformation can't be undertaken by the company's top team alone. The new kind of leadership that we've been advocating will have to cascade downward to build leadership muscle throughout the organization. But the place to start is in the C-suite. Surround yourself with talented people who can balance seemingly paradoxical leadership behaviors and challenge one another to collectively accomplish big things. Most importantly, make sure your leadership team truly leads—setting aside the time and energy to define a bold agenda and launch the ambitious initiatives that your future relies on. Failing to do that will be a costly mistake. Succeed and you will have a powerful team that can position your firm to thrive in an increasingly complex world.

Originally published in January–February 2022. Reprint R2201C

A Smarter Way to Network

by Rob Cross and Robert Thomas

ONE OF THE HAPPIEST, MOST SUCCESSFUL EXECUTIVES we know is a woman named Deb. She works at a major technology company and runs a global business unit that has more than 7,000 employees. When you ask her how she rose to the top and why she enjoys her job, her answer is simple: people. She points to her boss, the CEO, a mentor who "always has her back"; Steve, the head of a complementary business, with whom she has monthly brainstorming lunches and occasional gripe sessions; and Tom, a protégé to whom she has delegated responsibility for a large portion of her division. Outside the company, Deb's circle includes her counterparts in three strategic partnerships, who inspire her with new ideas; Sheila, a former colleague, now in a different industry, who gives her candid feedback; and her husband, Bob, an executive at a philanthropic organization. She also has close relationships with her fellow volunteers in a program for at-risk high school students and the members of her tennis group and book club.

This is Deb's social network (the real-world kind, not the virtual kind), and it has helped her career a lot. But not because the group is large or full of high-powered contacts. Her network is effective because it both supports and challenges her. Deb's relationships help her gain influence, broaden her expertise, learn new skills, and find purpose and balance. Deb values and nurtures them. "Make friends so that you have friends when you need friends" is her motto.

"My current role is really a product of a relationship I formed over a decade ago that came back to me at the right time," she explains. "People may chalk it up to luck, but I think more often than not luck happens through networks where people give first and are authentic in all they do."

Over the past 15 years, we've worked with many executives like Deb, at more than 300 companies. What began as organizational research—helping management teams understand and capitalize on the formal and informal social networks of their employees—has since metamorphosed into personal programs, which teach individual executives to increase their effectiveness by leveraging their networks.

The old adage "It's not what you know, it's who you know" is true. But it's more nuanced than that. In spite of what most self-help books say, network size doesn't usually matter. In fact, we've found that individuals who simply know a lot of people are less likely to achieve standout performance, because they're spread too thin. Political animals with lots of connections to corporate and industry leaders don't win the day, either. Yes, it's important to know powerful people, but if they account for too much of your network, your peers and subordinates often perceive you to be overly self-interested, and you may lose support as a result.

The data we've collected points to a different model for networking. The executives who consistently rank in the top 20% of their companies in both performance and well-being have diverse but select networks like Deb's—made up of high-quality relationships with people who come from several different spheres and from up and down the corporate hierarchy. These high performers, we have found, tap into six critical kinds of connections, which enhance their careers and lives in a variety of ways.

Through our work advising individual managers, we've also identified a four-step process that will help any executive develop this kind of network. But first, let's take a look at some common networking mistakes.

Idea in Brief

The adage "It's not what you know, it's who you know" is true. The right social network can have a huge impact on your success. But many people misunderstand what makes a network strong: They believe the key is maintaining a large circle filled with high-powered contacts. That's not the right approach, say Rob Cross, of UVA's McIntire School of Commerce, and Robert Thomas, of the Accenture Institute for High Performance. The authors, whose research looks at how organizations can capitalize on employees' social networks, have seen how the networks of the happiest, highest-performing executives are different: They're select but diverse, made up of high-quality relationships with people who come from varying spheres and from up and down the corporate ladder.

Effective networks typically range in size from 12 to 18 people. They help managers learn, make decisions with less bias, and grow personally. Cross and Thomas have found that they include six criti-cal kinds of connections: people who provide information, ideas, or expertise; formally and informally powerful people, who offer mentoring and political support; people who give developmental feedback; people who lend personal support; people who increase your sense of purpose or worth; and people who promote work-life balance. Moreover, the best kind of connections are "energizers"—positive, trustworthy individuals who enjoy other people and always see opportunities, even in challenging situations.

If your network doesn't look like this, you can follow a four-step process to improve it. You'll need to identify who your connections are and what they offer you, back away from redundant and energy-draining connections, fill holes in your network with the right kind of people, and work to make the most of your contacts. Do this, and in due course, you'll have a network that steers the best opportunities, ideas, and talent your way.

Getting It Wrong

Many people take a misguided approach to networking. They go astray by building imbalanced networks, pursuing the wrong kind of relationships, or leveraging relationships ineffectively. (See the sidebar "Are You Networking Impaired?") These people might remain

Are You Networking Impaired?

IN OUR WORK, WE HAVE IDENTIFIED six common managerial types who get stuck in three kinds of network traps. Do any of the descriptions below fit you?

The wrong structure

The formalist focuses too heavily on his company's official hierarchy, missing out on the efficiencies and opportunities that come from informal connections.

The overloaded manager has so much contact with colleagues and external ties that she becomes a bottleneck to progress and burns herself out.

The wrong relationships

The disconnected expert sticks with people who keep him focused on safe, existing competencies, rather than those who push him to build new skills.

The biased leader relies on advisers much like herself (same functional background, location, or values), who reinforce her biases, when she should instead seek outsiders to prompt more fully informed decisions.

The wrong behavior

The superficial networker engages in surface-level interaction with as many people as possible, mistakenly believing that a bigger network is a better one.

The chameleon changes his interests, values, and personality to match those of whatever subgroup is his audience, and winds up being disconnected from every group.

---

successful for a time, but often they will hit a plateau or see their career derailed because their networks couldn't prompt or support a critical transition.

Consider Dan, the chief information officer of one of the world's largest life-sciences organizations. He was under constant pressure to find new technologies that would spur innovation and speed the drug commercialization process at his company, and he needed a network that would help him. Unfortunately, more than 70% of his trusted advisers were in the unit he had worked in before becoming CIO. Not only did they reinforce his bias toward certain solutions and vendors, but they lacked the outside knowledge he needed. "I had started to mistake friendship, trust, and accessibility for real expertise in new domains," he told us. "This didn't mean I was going to dump these people, as they played important roles for me in other ways. But I needed to be more targeted in who I let influence my thinking."

Another overarching mistake we often see in executives' networks is an imbalance between connections that promote career advancement and those that promote engagement and satisfaction. Numerous studies have shown that happier executives are higher-performing ones.

Take Tim, the director of a large practice area at a leading professional services firm. On the surface he was doing well, but job stress had taken its toll. He was 40 pounds overweight, with alarmingly high cholesterol and blood sugar levels, and prone to extreme mood swings. When things went well at work, he was happy; when they didn't, he wasn't pleasant to be around. In fact, Tim's wife finally broke down and told him she thought he had become a career-obsessed jerk and needed to get other interests. With her encouragement, he joined Habitat for Humanity and started rowing with their daughter. As a result, his social network expanded to include people with different perspectives and values, who helped him focus on more healthful and fulfilling pursuits. "As I spent more time with different groups, what I cared about diversified," he says. "Physically, I'm in much better shape and probably staved off a heart attack. But I think I'm a better leader, too, in that I think about problems more broadly, and I'm more resilient. Our peer feedback systems are also clearly indicating that people are more committed to the new me."

Getting It Right

To understand more about what makes an effective network, let's look again at Deb. She has a small set of core contacts—14 people she really relies on. Effective core networks typically range in size from 12 to 18 people. But what really matters is structure: Core connections must bridge smaller, more-diverse kinds of groups and cross hierarchical, organizational, functional, and geographic lines. Core relationships should result in more learning, less bias in decision-making, and greater personal growth and balance. The people in your inner circle should also model positive behaviors, because if those around you are enthusiastic, authentic, and generous, you will be, too.

More specifically, our data shows that high performers have strong ties to:

- People who offer them new information or expertise, including internal or external clients, who increase their market awareness; peers in other functions, divisions, or geographies, who share best practices; and contacts in other industries, who inspire innovation

- Formally powerful people, who provide mentoring, sense-making, political support, and resources; and informally powerful people, who offer influence, help coordinating projects, and support among the rank and file

- People who give them developmental feedback, challenge their decisions, and push them to be better. At an early career stage, an employee might get this from a boss or customers; later, it tends to come from coaches, trusted colleagues, or a spouse

Meanwhile, the most satisfied executives have ties to

- People who provide personal support, such as colleagues who help them get back on track when they're having a bad day or friends with whom they can just be themselves

- People who add a sense of purpose or worth, such as bosses and customers who validate their work, and family members and other stakeholders who show them work has a broader meaning

- People who promote their work-life balance, holding them accountable for activities that improve their physical health (such as sports), mental engagement (such as hobbies or educational classes), or spiritual well-being (music, religion, art, or volunteer work)

How does one create such a varied network? We recommend a four-point action plan: analyze, de-layer, diversify, and capitalize.

Analyze

Start by looking at the individuals in your network. Where are they located—are they within your team, your unit, or your company, or

---

Four steps to building a better network

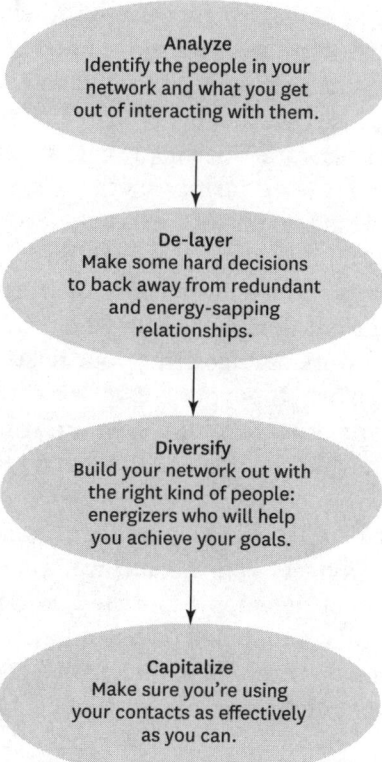

Analyze
Identify the people in your
network and what you get
out of interacting with them.

De-layer
Make some hard decisions
to back away from redundant
and energy-sapping
relationships.

Diversify
Build your network out with
the right kind of people:
energizers who will help
you achieve your goals.

Capitalize
Make sure you're using
your contacts as effectively
as you can.

---

outside your organization? What benefits do your interactions with them provide? How energizing are those interactions?

The last question is an important one. Energizers bring out the best in everyone around them, and our data shows that having them in your network is a strong predictor of success over time. These people aren't necessarily extroverted or charismatic. They're people who always see opportunities, even in challenging situations, and create room for others to meaningfully contribute. Good energizers are trustworthy and committed to principles larger than their self-interest, and they enjoy other people. "De-energizers," by contrast, are quick to point out obstacles, critique people rather than ideas, are inflexible in their thinking, fail to create opportunities, miss commitments, and don't show concern for others. Unfortunately, energy-sapping interactions have more impact than energizing ones—up to seven times as much, according to one study. And our own research suggests that roughly 90% of anxiety at work is created by 5% of one's network—the people who sap energy.

Next, classify your relationships by the benefits they provide. Generally, benefits fall into one of six basic categories: information, political support and influence, personal development, personal support and energy, a sense of purpose or worth, and work-life balance. It's important to have people who provide each kind of benefit in your network. Categorizing your relationships will give you a clearer idea of whether your network is extending your abilities or keeping you stuck. You'll see where you have holes and redundancies and which people you depend on too much—or not enough.

Let's use Joe, a rising star in an investment bank, as a case study. He had 24 close advisers—on the surface, a more than healthy number. But many of the people he relied on were from his own department and frequently relied on one another. If he eliminated those redundancies, his network shrank to five people. After giving it some thought and observing his peers' networks, he realized he was missing links with several important types of people: colleagues focused on financial offerings outside his own products, who could help him deliver broader financial solutions to customers; coworkers in different geographies—particularly London and Asia—who could enhance his ability to sell to global clients; and board-level relationships at key accounts, who could make client introductions and influence purchasing decisions. His insularity was limiting his options and hurting his chances of promotion to managing director. He realized he would need to focus on cultivating a network rather than allowing it to organically arise from the day-to-day demands of his work.

De-layer

Once you've analyzed your network, you need to make some hard decisions about which relationships to back away from. First, look at eliminating or minimizing contact with people who sap you of energy or promote unhealthful behaviors. You can do this by reshaping your role to avoid them, devoting less time to them, working to change their behavior, or reframing your reactions so that you don't dwell on the interactions.

John, an academic, realized that two university administrators in his network were causing him a great deal of anxiety. This had so soured his view of his school that he was considering leaving. He therefore decided to devote less time to projects and committees that would involve the negative contacts and to avoid dwelling on any sniping comments they subjected him to. Within a year he was much more productive and happy. "By shifting my role and how I reacted to the idiots, I turned a negative situation around," John says. "In hindsight it was an obvious move—rather than leave a place I loved—but emotions can spiral on you in ways you don't recognize."

The next step is to ask yourself which of the six categories have too many people in them. Early-stage leaders, for example, tend to focus too much on information and not enough on personal development and might want to shed some of the contacts who give them the former to make more time for those who give them the latter.

Beyond this, consider which individuals—and types of people as determined by function, hierarchy, or geography—have too much of you, and why. Is the cause structural, in that work procedures require you to be involved? Or is your own behavior causing the imbalance? What can you change to rectify the situation? Too often we see leaders fail because they accept or create too many collaborative demands.

Paul, the head of research in a consumer products company, had a network of almost 70 people just at work. But he got many complaints from people who said they needed greater access to him. His productivity, and his unit's, was suffering. When he analyzed his network, he realized that he was missing "people and initiatives one or two levels out." To address this, he decided to delegate—stepping away from interactions that didn't require his presence and cultivating "go to" stand-ins in certain areas of expertise. He also changed his leadership style from extraordinarily accessible to helpful but more removed, which encouraged subordinates to solve their own problems by connecting with people around him. "As a leader you can find yourself in this bubble of activity where you feel like a lot is happening moving from meeting to meeting," Paul says. "You can actually start to thrive on this in some ways. I had to move past this for us to be effective as a unit and so that I could be more forward-thinking."

Diversify

Now that you've created room in your network, you need to fill it with the right people. Simple tools like worksheets can help you get started. For example, you might make a list of the six categories of relationships and think about colleagues who could fill the holes you have in each. Remember to focus on positive, energetic, selfless people, and be sure to ask people inside and outside your network for recommendations.

You should also think about how you could connect your network to your professional and personal goals. Here's another simple exercise: Write down three specific business results you hope to achieve over the next year (such as doubling sales or winning an Asia-based client) and then list the people (by name or general role) who could help you with them, thanks to their expertise, control over resources, or ability to provide political support. Joe, the investment banker, identified counterparts in the Asian and European operations of his company who had relationships with the clients he was focused on and then scheduled regular calls with them to coordinate efforts. "In a couple of cases this helped me identify opportunities I could pitch proactively. In others it just helped us appear more coordinated when we were competing against other banks," he says. One of the big challenges for Paul, the consumer products executive, was managing a new facility and line of innovation in China. Because none of his trusted advisers had ever even been to that country, he reached out to the head of R&D at a major life-sciences organization that had undertaken a similar effort.

Capitalize

Last, make sure you're using your contacts as effectively as you can. Are there people you rely on in one sphere, such as political support, that you could also use to fill a need in another, such as personal development? Could you get more out of some relationships if you put more energy into them? Our research shows, for instance, that high performers at all levels tend to use their information contacts to gain other benefits, such as new ideas. Reciprocal relationships also tend to be more fruitful; the most successful leaders always look for ways to give more to their contacts.

Alan, a top executive at a global insurance company, realized that although he had a good network, he was still making decisions in relative isolation. He failed to elicit insights from others and, as a result, wasn't making enough progress toward his goals. So he started inviting his more-junior contacts, who were informal opinion leaders in his company, to lunch and asking them open-ended questions. These conversations led him to streamline decision-making and uncover innovation deep within the firm's hierarchy. "When I met with one lady, I was stunned at a great new product idea she had been pushing for months," Alan says. "But she hadn't been able to get the right people to listen. I was able to step in and help make things happen. To me the right way to be tapping into people is in this exploratory way—whether it is about strategic insights or just

Never worry alone – DB

how they think I'm doing on some aspect of my job. That's how I get to new ways of thinking and doing things, and I know it makes me much more effective than people who are smarter than me."

A network constructed using this four-point model will build on itself over time. In due course, it will ensure that the best opportunities, ideas, and talent come your way.

Originally published in July–August 2011. Reprint R1107P

Leadership That Gets Results

by Daniel Goleman

ASK ANY GROUP OF businesspeople the question "What do effective leaders do?" and you'll hear a sweep of answers. Leaders set strategy; they motivate; they create a mission; they build a culture. Then ask "What *should* leaders do?" If the group is seasoned, you'll likely hear one response: The leader's singular job is to get results.

But how? The mystery of what leaders can and ought to do in order to spark the best performance from their people is age-old. In recent years, that mystery has spawned an entire cottage industry: Literally thousands of "leadership experts" have made careers of testing and coaching executives, all in pursuit of creating businesspeople who can turn bold objectives—be they strategic, financial, organizational, or all three—into reality.

Still, effective leadership eludes many people and organizations. One reason is that until recently, virtually no quantitative research has demonstrated which precise leadership behaviors yield positive results. Leadership experts proffer advice based on inference, experience, and instinct. Sometimes that advice is right on target; sometimes it's not.

But new research by the consulting firm Hay/McBer, which draws on a random sample of 3,871 executives selected from a database of more than 20,000 executives worldwide, takes much of the mystery out of effective leadership. The research found six distinct leadership styles, each springing from different components of emotional intelligence. The styles, taken individually, appear to have a direct and unique impact on the working atmosphere of a company, division, or team, and in turn, on its financial performance. And perhaps most important, the research indicates that leaders with the best results do not rely on only one leadership style; they use most of them in a given week—seamlessly and in different measure—depending on the business situation. Imagine the styles, then, as the array of clubs in a golf pro's bag. Over the course of a game, the pro picks and chooses clubs based on the demands of the shot. Sometimes he has to ponder his selection, but usually it is automatic. The pro senses the challenge ahead, swiftly pulls out the right tool, and elegantly puts it to work. That's how high-impact leaders operate, too.

What are the six styles of leadership? None will shock workplace veterans. Indeed, each style, by name and brief description alone, will likely resonate with anyone who leads, is led, or as is the case with most of us, does both. *Coercive leaders* demand immediate compliance. *Authoritative leaders* mobilize people toward a vision. *Affiliative leaders* create emotional bonds and harmony. *Democratic leaders* build consensus through participation. *Pacesetting leaders* expect excellence and self-direction. And *coaching leaders* develop people for the future.

Close your eyes and you can surely imagine a colleague who uses any one of these styles. You most likely use at least one yourself. What is new in this research, then, is its implications for action. First, it offers a fine-grained understanding of how different leadership styles affect performance and results. Second, it offers clear guidance on when a manager should switch between them. It also strongly suggests that switching flexibly is well advised. New, too, is the research's finding that each leadership style springs from different components of emotional intelligence.

Idea in Brief

Many managers mistakenly assume that leadership style is a function of personality rather than strategic choice. Instead of choosing the one style that suits their temperament, they should ask which style best addresses the demands of a particular situation.

Research has shown that the most successful leaders have strengths in the following emotional intelligence competencies:

self-awareness, self-regulation, motivation, empathy, and social skill. There are six basic styles of leadership; each makes use of the key components of emotional intelligence in different combinations. The best leaders don't know just one style of leadership—they're skilled at several, and have the flexibility to switch between styles as the circumstances dictate.

Measuring Leadership's Impact

It has been more than a decade since research first linked aspects of emotional intelligence to business results. The late David McClelland, a noted Harvard University psychologist, found that leaders with strengths in a critical mass of six or more emotional intelligence competencies were far more effective than peers who lacked such strengths. For instance, when he analyzed the performance of division heads at a global food and beverage company, he found that among leaders with this critical mass of competence, 87% placed in the top third for annual salary bonuses based on their business performance. More telling, their divisions on average outperformed yearly revenue targets by 15% to 20%. Those executives who lacked emotional intelligence were rarely rated as outstanding in their annual performance reviews, and their divisions underperformed by an average of almost 20%.

Our research set out to gain a more molecular view of the links among leadership and emotional intelligence, and climate and performance. A team of McClelland's colleagues headed by Mary Fontaine and Ruth Jacobs from Hay/McBer studied data about or observed thousands of executives, noting specific behaviors and their impact on climate.[1] How did each individual motivate direct

Idea in Practice

Managers often fail to appreciate how profoundly the organizational climate can influence financial results. It can account for nearly a third of financial performance. Organizational climate, in turn, is influenced by leadership style—by the way that managers motivate direct reports, gather and use information, make decisions, manage change initiatives, and handle crises. There are six basic leadership styles. Each derives from different emotional intelligence competencies, works best in particular situations, and affects the organizational climate in different ways.

1. **The coercive style.** This "Do what I say" approach can be very effective in a turnaround situation, a natural disaster, or when working with problem employees. But in most situations, coercive leadership inhibits the organization's flexibility and dampens employees' motivation.

2. **The authoritative style.** An authoritative leader takes a "Come with me" approach: She states the overall goal but gives people the freedom to choose their own means of achieving it. This style works especially well when a business is adrift. It is less effective when the leader is working with a team of experts who are more experienced than he is.

3. **The affiliative style.** The hallmark of the affiliative leader is a "people come first" attitude. This style is particularly useful for building team harmony or increasing morale. But its exclusive focus on praise can allow poor performance to go

reports? Manage change initiatives? Handle crises? It was in a later phase of the research that we identified which emotional intelligence capabilities drive the six leadership styles. How does the leader rate in terms of self-control and social skill? Does he show high or low levels of empathy?

The team tested each executive's immediate sphere of influence for its climate. "Climate" is not an amorphous term. First defined by psychologists George Litwin and Richard Stringer and later refined by McClelland and his colleagues, it refers to six key factors that influence an organization's working environment: its *flexibility*—that is, how free employees feel to innovate unencumbered by red tape; their sense of *responsibility* to the organization; the level of uncorrected. Also, affiliative leaders rarely offer advice, which often leaves employees in a quandary.

4. **The democratic style.** This style's impact on organizational climate is not as high as you might imagine. By giving workers a voice in decisions, democratic leaders build organizational flexibility and responsibility and help generate fresh ideas. But sometimes the price is endless meetings and confused employees who feel leaderless.

5. **The pacesetting style.** A leader who sets high performance standards and exemplifies them himself has a very positive impact on employees who are self-motivated and highly competent. But other employees tend to feel overwhelmed by such a leader's demands for excellence—and to resent his tendency to take over a situation.

6. **The coaching style.** This style focuses more on personal development than on immediate work-related tasks. It works well when employees are already aware of their weaknesses and want to improve, but not when they are resistant to changing their ways.

The more styles a leader has mastered, the better. In particular, being able to switch among the authoritative, affiliative, democratic, and coaching styles as conditions dictate creates the best organizational climate and optimizes business performance.

standards that people set; the sense of accuracy about performance feedback and aptness of *rewards*; the *clarity* people have about mission and values; and finally, the level of *commitment* to a common purpose.

We found that all six leadership styles have a measurable effect on each aspect of climate. (For details, see the exhibit "Getting molecular: The impact of leadership styles on drivers of climate.") Further, when we looked at the impact of climate on financial results—such as return on sales, revenue growth, efficiency, and profitability—we found a direct correlation between the two. Leaders who used styles that positively affected the climate had decidedly better financial results than those who did not. That is not to say that organizational climate is the only driver of performance. Economic conditions and competitive dynamics matter enormously. But our analysis strongly suggests that climate accounts for nearly a third of results. And that's simply too much of an impact to ignore.

The Styles in Detail

Executives use six leadership styles, but only four of the six consistently have a positive effect on climate and results. Let's look then at each style of leadership in detail. (For a summary of the material that follows, see the chart "The six leadership styles at a glance.")

The coercive style

The computer company was in crisis mode—its sales and profits were falling, its stock was losing value precipitously, and its shareholders were in an uproar. The board brought in a new CEO with a reputation as a turnaround artist. He set to work chopping jobs, selling off divisions, and making the tough decisions that should have been executed years before. The company was saved, at least in the short term.

From the start, though, the CEO created a reign of terror, bullying and demeaning his executives, roaring his displeasure at the slightest misstep. The company's top echelons were decimated not just by his erratic firings but also by defections. The CEO's direct reports, frightened by his tendency to blame the bearer of bad news, stopped bringing him any news at all. Morale was at an all-time low—a fact reflected in another downturn in the business after the short-term recovery. The CEO was eventually fired by the board of directors.

It's easy to understand why of all the leadership styles, the coercive one is the least effective in most situations. Consider what the style does to an organization's climate. Flexibility is the hardest hit. The leader's extreme top-down decision-making kills new ideas on the vine. People feel so disrespected that they think, "I won't even bring my ideas up—they'll only be shot down." Likewise, people's sense of responsibility evaporates: Unable to act on their own initiative, they lose their sense of ownership and feel little accountability for their performance. Some become so resentful they adopt the attitude, "I'm not going to help this bastard."

Coercive leadership also has a damaging effect on the rewards system. Most high-performing workers are motivated by more than money—they seek the satisfaction of work well done. The coercive style erodes such pride. And finally, the style undermines one of the leader's prime tools—motivating people by showing them how their job fits into a grand, shared mission. Such a loss, measured in terms of diminished clarity and commitment, leaves people alienated from their own jobs, wondering, "How does any of this matter?"

Given the impact of the coercive style, you might assume it should never be applied. Our research, however, uncovered a few occasions when it worked masterfully. Take the case of a division president who was brought in to change the direction of a food company that was losing money. His first act was to have the executive conference room demolished. To him, the room—with its long marble table that looked like "the deck of the Starship *Enterprise*"—symbolized the tradition-bound formality that was paralyzing the company. The destruction of the room, and the subsequent move to a smaller, more informal setting, sent a message no one could miss, and the division's culture changed quickly in its wake.

That said, the coercive style should be used only with extreme caution and in the few situations when it is absolutely imperative, such as during a turnaround or when a hostile takeover is looming. In those cases, the coercive style can break failed business habits and shock people into new ways of working. It is always appropriate during a genuine emergency, like in the aftermath of an earthquake or a fire. And it can work with problem employees with whom all else has failed. But if a leader relies solely on this style or continues to use it once the emergency passes, the long-term impact of his insensitivity to the morale and feelings of those he leads will be ruinous.

The authoritative style

Tom was the vice president of marketing at a floundering national restaurant chain that specialized in pizza. Needless to say, the

Emotional Intelligence: A Primer

EMOTIONAL INTELLIGENCE—the ability to manage ourselves and our relationships effectively—consists of four fundamental capabilities: self-awareness, self-management, social awareness, and social skill. Each capability, in turn, is composed of specific sets of competencies. Below is a list of the capabilities and their corresponding traits.

Self-Awareness

- *Emotional self-awareness:* the ability to read and understand your emotions as well as recognize their impact on work performance, relationships, and the like.

- *Accurate self-assessment:* a realistic evaluation of your strengths and limitations.

- *Self-confidence:* a strong and positive sense of self-worth.

Self-Management

- *Self-control:* the ability to keep disruptive emotions and impulses under control.

- *Trustworthiness:* a consistent display of honesty and integrity.

- *Conscientiousness:* the ability to manage yourself and your responsibilities.

- *Adaptability:* skill at adjusting to changing situations and overcoming obstacles.

- *Achievement orientation:* the drive to meet an internal standard of excellence.

- *Initiative:* a readiness to seize opportunities.

---

company's poor performance troubled the senior managers, but they were at a loss for what to do. Every Monday, they met to review recent sales, struggling to come up with fixes. To Tom, the approach didn't make sense. "We were always trying to figure out why our sales were down last week. We had the whole company looking backward instead of figuring out what we had to do tomorrow."

Tom saw an opportunity to change people's way of thinking at an off-site strategy meeting. There, the conversation began with stale truisms: The company had to drive up shareholder wealth and

Social Awareness

- *Empathy:* skill at sensing other people's emotions, understanding their perspective, and taking an active interest in their concerns.

- *Organizational awareness:* the ability to read the currents of organizational life, build decision networks, and navigate politics.

- *Service orientation:* the ability to recognize and meet customers' needs.

Social Skill

- *Visionary leadership:* the ability to take charge and inspire with a compelling vision.

- *Influence:* the ability to wield a range of persuasive tactics.

- *Developing others:* the propensity to bolster the abilities of others through feedback and guidance.

- *Communication:* skill at listening and at sending clear, convincing, and well-tuned messages.

- *Change catalyst:* proficiency in initiating new ideas and leading people in a new direction.

- *Conflict management:* the ability to de-escalate disagreements and orchestrate resolutions.

- *Building bonds:* proficiency at cultivating and maintaining a web of relationships.

- *Teamwork and collaboration:* competence at promoting cooperation and building teams.

---

increase return on assets. Tom believed those concepts didn't have the power to inspire a restaurant manager to be innovative or to do better than a good-enough job.

So Tom made a bold move. In the middle of a meeting, he made an impassioned plea for his colleagues to think from the customer's perspective. Customers want convenience, he said. The company was not in the restaurant business; it was in the business of distributing high-quality, convenient-to-get pizza. That notion—and nothing else—should drive everything the company did.

Getting molecular: The impact of leadership styles on drivers of climate

Our research investigated how each leadership style affected the six drivers of climate, or working atmosphere. The figures below show the correlation between each leadership style and each aspect of climate. So, for instance, if we look at the climate driver of flexibility, we see that the coercive style has a –.28 correlation while the democratic style has a .28 correlation, equally strong in the opposite direction. Focusing on the authoritative leadership style, we find that it has a .54 correlation with rewards—strongly positive—and a .21 correlation with responsibility—positive, but not as strong. In other words, the style's correlation with rewards was more than twice that with responsibility.

According to the data, the authoritative leadership style has the most positive effect on climate, but three others— affiliative, democratic, and coaching—follow close behind. That said, the research indicates that no style should be relied on exclusively, and all have at least short-term uses.

	Coercive	Authoritative	Affiliative	Democratic	Pacesetting	Coaching
Flexibility	–.28	.32	.27	.28	–.07	.17
Responsibility	–.37	.21	.16	.23	.04	.08
Standards	.02	.38	.31	.22	–.27	.39
Rewards	–.18	.54	.48	.42	–.29	.43
Clarity	–.11	.44	.37	.35	–.28	.38
Commitment	–.13	.35	.34	.26	–.20	.27
Overall impact on climate	–.26	.54	.46	.43	–.25	.42

With his vibrant enthusiasm and clear vision—the hallmarks of the authoritative style—Tom filled a leadership vacuum at the company. Indeed, his concept became the core of the new mission statement. But this conceptual breakthrough was just the beginning. Tom made sure that the mission statement was built into the company's strategic planning process as the designated driver of growth. And he ensured that the vision was articulated so that local restaurant managers understood they were the key to the company's success and were free to find new ways to distribute pizza.

Changes came quickly. Within weeks, many local managers started guaranteeing fast, new delivery times. Even better, they started to act like entrepreneurs, finding ingenious locations to open new branches: kiosks on busy street corners and in bus and train stations, even from carts in airports and hotel lobbies.

Tom's success was no fluke. Our research indicates that of the six leadership styles, the authoritative one is most effective, driving up every aspect of climate. Take clarity. The authoritative leader is a visionary; he motivates people by making clear to them how their work fits into a larger vision for the organization. People who work for such leaders understand that what they do matters and why. Authoritative leadership also maximizes commitment to the organization's goals and strategy. By framing the individual tasks within a grand vision, the authoritative leader defines standards that revolve around that vision. When he gives performance feedback—whether positive or negative—the singular criterion is whether or not that performance furthers the vision. The standards for success are clear to all, as are the rewards. Finally, consider the style's impact on flexibility. An authoritative leader states the end but generally gives people plenty of leeway to devise their own means. Authoritative leaders give people the freedom to innovate, experiment, and take calculated risks.

Because of its positive impact, the authoritative style works well in almost any business situation. But it is particularly effective when a business is adrift. An authoritative leader charts a new course and sells his people on a fresh long-term vision.

The authoritative style, powerful though it may be, will not work in every situation. The approach fails, for instance, when a leader is working with a team of experts or peers who are more experienced than he is; they may see the leader as pompous or out of touch. Another limitation: If a manager trying to be authoritative becomes overbearing, he can undermine the egalitarian spirit of an effective team. Yet even with such caveats, leaders would be wise to grab for the authoritative "club" more often than not. It may not guarantee a hole in one, but it certainly helps with the long drive.

The affiliative style

If the coercive leader demands, "Do what I say," and the authoritative urges, "Come with me," the affiliative leader says, "People come first." This leadership style revolves around people—its proponents value individuals and their emotions more than tasks and goals. The affiliative leader strives to keep employees happy and to create harmony among them. He manages by building strong emotional bonds and then reaping the benefits of such an approach, namely fierce loyalty. The style also has a markedly positive effect on communication. People who like one another a lot talk a lot. They share ideas; they share inspiration. And the style drives up flexibility; friends trust one another, allowing habitual innovation and risk-taking. Flexibility also rises because the affiliative leader, like a parent who adjusts household rules for a maturing adolescent, doesn't impose unnecessary strictures on how employees get their work done. They give people the freedom to do their job in the way they think is most effective.

As for a sense of recognition and reward for work well done, the affiliative leader offers ample positive feedback. Such feedback has special potency in the workplace because it is all too rare: Outside of an annual review, most people usually get no feedback on their day-to-day efforts—or only negative feedback. That makes the affiliative leader's positive words all the more motivating. Finally, affiliative leaders are masters at building a sense of belonging. They are, for instance, likely to take their direct reports out for a meal or a drink, one-on-one, to see how they're doing. They will bring in a cake to celebrate a group accomplishment. They are natural relationship builders.

Joe Torre, the heart and soul of the New York Yankees, is a classic affiliative leader. During the 1999 World Series, Torre tended ably to the psyches of his players as they endured the emotional pressure cooker of a pennant race. All season long, he made a special point to praise Scott Brosius, whose father had died during the season, for staying committed even as he mourned. At the celebration party after the team's final game, Torre specifically sought out right fielder Paul O'Neill. Although he had received the news of his father's death that morning, O'Neill chose to play in the decisive game— and he burst into tears the moment it ended. Torre made a point of acknowledging O'Neill's personal struggle, calling him a "warrior." Torre also used the spotlight of the victory celebration to praise two players whose return the following year was threatened by contract disputes. In doing so, he sent a clear message to the team and to the club's owner that he valued the players immensely—too much to lose them.

Along with ministering to the emotions of his people, an affiliative leader may also tend to his own emotions openly. The year Torre's brother was near death awaiting a heart transplant, he shared his worries with his players. He also spoke candidly with the team about his treatment for prostate cancer.

The affiliative style's generally positive impact makes it a good all-weather approach, but leaders should employ it particularly when trying to build team harmony, increase morale, improve communication, or repair broken trust. For instance, one executive in our study was hired to replace a ruthless team leader. The former leader had taken credit for his employees' work and had attempted to pit them against one another. His efforts ultimately failed, but the team he left behind was suspicious and weary. The new executive managed to mend the situation by unstintingly showing emotional honesty and rebuilding ties. Several months in, her leadership had created a renewed sense of commitment and energy.

Despite its benefits, the affiliative style should not be used alone. Its exclusive focus on praise can allow poor performance to go

The six leadership styles at a glance

Our research found that leaders use six styles, each springing from different components of emotional intelligence. Here is a summary of the styles, their origins, when they work best, and their impact on an organization's climate and thus its performance.

	Coercive	Authoritative
The leader's modus operandi	Demands immediate compliance	Mobilizes people toward a vision
The style in a phrase	"Do what I tell you."	"Come with me."
Underlying emotional intelligence competencies	Drive to achieve, initiative, self-control	Self-confidence, empathy, change catalyst
When the style works best	In a crisis, to kick-start a turnaround, or with problem employees	When changes require a new vision, or when a clear direction is needed
Overall impact on climate	Negative	Most strongly positive

uncorrected; employees may perceive that mediocrity is tolerated. And because affiliative leaders rarely offer constructive advice on how to improve, employees must figure out how to do so on their own. When people need clear directives to navigate through complex challenges, the affiliative style leaves them rudderless. Indeed, if overly relied on, this style can actually steer a group to failure. Perhaps that is why many affiliative leaders, including Torre, use this style in close conjunction with the authoritative style. Authoritative leaders state a vision, set standards, and let people know how their work is furthering the group's goals. Alternate that with the caring, nurturing approach of the affiliative leader, and you have a potent combination.

Affiliative	Democratic	Pacesetting	Coaching
Creates harmony and builds emotional bonds	Forges consensus through participation	Sets high standards for performance	Develops people for the future
"People come first."	"What do you think?"	"Do as I do—now."	"Try this."
Empathy, building relationships, communication	Collaboration, team leadership, communication	Conscientiousness, drive to achieve, initiative	Developing others, empathy, self-awareness
To heal rifts in a team or to motivate people during stressful circumstances	To build buy-in or consensus, or to get input from valuable employees	To get quick results from a highly motivated and competent team	To help an employee improve performance or develop long-term strengths
Positive	Positive	Negative	Positive

The democratic style

Sister Mary ran a Catholic school system in a large metropolitan area. One of the schools—the only private school in an impoverished neighborhood—had been losing money for years, and the archdiocese could no longer afford to keep it open. When Sister Mary eventually got the order to shut it down, she didn't just lock the doors. She called a meeting of all the teachers and staff at the school and explained to them the details of the financial crisis—the first time anyone working at the school had been included in the business side of the institution. She asked for their ideas on ways to keep the school open and on how to handle the closing, should it come to that. Sister Mary spent much of her time at the meeting just listening.

She did the same at later meetings for school parents and for the community and during a successive series of meetings for the school's teachers and staff. After two months of meetings, the consensus was clear: The school would have to close. A plan was made to transfer students to other schools in the Catholic system.

The final outcome was no different than if Sister Mary had gone ahead and closed the school the day she was told to. But by allowing the school's constituents to reach that decision collectively, Sister Mary received none of the backlash that would have accompanied such a move. People mourned the loss of the school, but they understood its inevitability. Virtually no one objected.

Compare that with the experiences of a priest in our research who headed another Catholic school. He, too, was told to shut it down. And he did—by fiat. The result was disastrous: Parents filed lawsuits, teachers and parents picketed, and local newspapers ran editorials attacking his decision. It took a year to resolve the disputes before he could finally go ahead and close the school.

Sister Mary exemplifies the democratic style in action—and its benefits. By spending time getting people's ideas and buy-in, a leader builds trust, respect, and commitment. By letting workers themselves have a say in decisions that affect their goals and how they do their work, the democratic leader drives up flexibility and responsibility. And by listening to employees' concerns, the democratic leader learns what to do to keep morale high. Finally, because they have a say in setting their goals and the standards for evaluating success, people operating in a democratic system tend to be very realistic about what can and cannot be accomplished.

However, the democratic style has its drawbacks, which is why its impact on climate is not as high as some of the other styles. One of its more exasperating consequences can be endless meetings where ideas are mulled over, consensus remains elusive, and the only visible result is scheduling more meetings. Some democratic leaders use the style to put off making crucial decisions, hoping that enough thrashing things out will eventually yield a blinding insight. In reality, their people end up feeling confused and leaderless. Such an approach can even escalate conflicts.

When does the style work best? This approach is ideal when a leader is himself uncertain about the best direction to take and needs ideas and guidance from able employees. And even if a leader has a strong vision, the democratic style works well to generate fresh ideas for executing that vision.

The democratic style, of course, makes much less sense when employees are not competent or informed enough to offer sound advice. And it almost goes without saying that building consensus is wrongheaded in times of crisis. Take the case of a CEO whose computer company was severely threatened by changes in the market. He always sought consensus about what to do. As competitors stole customers and customers' needs changed, he kept appointing committees to consider the situation. When the market made a sudden shift because of a new technology, the CEO froze in his tracks. The board replaced him before he could appoint yet another task force to consider the situation. The new CEO, while occasionally democratic and affiliative, relied heavily on the authoritative style, especially in his first months.

The pacesetting style
Like the coercive style, the pacesetting style has its place in the leader's repertory, but it should be used sparingly. That's not what we expected to find. After all, the hallmarks of the pacesetting style sound admirable. The leader sets extremely high performance standards and exemplifies them herself. She is obsessive about doing things better and faster, and she asks the same of everyone around him. She quickly pinpoints poor performers and demands more from them. If they don't rise to the occasion, she replaces them with people who can. You would think such an approach would improve results, but it doesn't.

In fact, the pacesetting style destroys climate. Many employees feel overwhelmed by the pacesetter's demands for excellence, and their morale drops. Guidelines for working may be clear in the leader's head, but she does not state them clearly; she expects people to know what to do and even thinks, "If I have to tell you, you're the wrong person for the job." Work becomes not a matter of doing one's best along a clear course so much as second-guessing what the leader wants. At the same time, people often feel that the pacesetter doesn't trust them to work in their own way or to take initiative. Flexibility and responsibility evaporate; work becomes so task focused and routinized it's boring.

As for rewards, the pacesetter either gives no feedback on how people are doing or jumps in to take over when he thinks they're lagging. And if the leader should leave, people feel directionless—they're so used to "the expert" setting the rules. Finally, commitment dwindles under the regime of a pacesetting leader because people have no sense of how their personal efforts fit into the big picture.

For an example of the pacesetting style, take the case of Sam, a biochemist in R&D at a large pharmaceutical company. Sam's superb technical expertise made him an early star: He was the one everyone turned to when they needed help. Soon he was promoted to head of a team developing a new product. The other scientists on the team were as competent and self-motivated as Sam; his métier as team leader became offering himself as a model of how to do first-class scientific work under tremendous deadline pressure, pitching in when needed. His team completed its task in record time.

But then came a new assignment: Sam was put in charge of R&D for his entire division. As his tasks expanded and he had to articulate a vision, coordinate projects, delegate responsibility, and help develop others, Sam began to slip. Not trusting that his subordinates were as capable as he was, he became a micromanager, obsessed with details and taking over for others when their performance slackened. Instead of trusting them to improve with guidance and development, Sam found himself working nights and weekends after stepping in to take over for the head of a floundering research team. Finally, his own boss suggested, to his relief, that he return to his old job as head of a product development team.

Although Sam faltered, the pacesetting style isn't always a disaster. The approach works well when all employees are self-motivated, highly competent, and need little direction or coordination—for example, it can work for leaders of highly skilled and self-motivated professionals, like R&D groups or legal teams. And, given a talented team to lead, pacesetting does exactly that: gets work done on time or even ahead of schedule. Yet like any leadership style, pacesetting should never be used by itself.

The coaching style

A product unit at a global computer company had seen sales plummet from twice as much as its competitors to only half as much. So Lawrence, the president of the manufacturing division, decided to close the unit and reassign its people and products. Upon hearing the news, James, the head of the doomed unit, decided to go over his boss's head and plead his case to the CEO.

What did Lawrence do? Instead of blowing up at James, he sat down with his rebellious direct report and talked over not just the decision to close the division but also James's future. He explained to James how moving to another division would help him develop new skills. It would make him a better leader and teach him more about the company's business.

Lawrence acted more like a counselor than a traditional boss. He listened to James's concerns and hopes, and he shared his own. He said he believed James had grown stale in his current job; it was, after all, the only place he'd worked in the company. He predicted that James would blossom in a new role.

The conversation then took a practical turn. James had not yet had his meeting with the CEO—the one he had impetuously demanded when he heard of his division's closing. Knowing this—and also knowing that the CEO unwaveringly supported the closing—Lawrence took the time to coach James on how to present his case in that meeting. "You don't get an audience with the CEO very often," he noted. "Let's make sure you impress him with your thoughtfulness." He advised James not to plead his personal case but to focus on the business unit: "If he thinks you're in there for your own glory, he'll throw you out faster than you walked through the door." And he urged him to put his ideas in writing; the CEO always appreciated that.

Lawrence's reason for coaching instead of scolding? "James is a good guy, very talented and promising," the executive explained to us, "and I don't want this to derail his career. I want him to stay with the company, I want him to work out, I want him to learn, I want him to benefit and grow. Just because he screwed up doesn't mean he's terrible."

Lawrence's actions illustrate the coaching style par excellence. Coaching leaders help employees identify their unique strengths and weaknesses and tie them to their personal and career aspirations. They encourage employees to establish long-term development goals and help them conceptualize a plan for attaining them. They make agreements with their employees about their role and responsibilities in enacting development plans, and they give plentiful instruction and feedback. Coaching leaders excel at delegating; they give employees challenging assignments, even if that means the tasks won't be accomplished quickly. In other words, these leaders are willing to put up with short-term failure if it furthers long-term learning.

Of the six styles, our research found that the coaching style is used least often. Many leaders told us they don't have the time in this high-pressure economy for the slow and tedious work of teaching people and helping them grow. But after a first session, it takes little or no extra time. Leaders who ignore this style are passing up a powerful tool: Its impact on climate and performance are markedly positive.

Admittedly, there is a paradox in coaching's positive effect on business performance because coaching focuses primarily on personal development, not on immediate work-related tasks. Even so, coaching improves results. The reason: It requires constant dialogue, and that dialogue has a way of pushing up every driver of climate. Take flexibility. When an employee knows his boss watches him and cares about what he does, he feels free to experiment. After all, he's sure to get quick and constructive feedback. Similarly, the ongoing dialogue of coaching guarantees that people know what is expected of them and how their work fits into a larger vision or strategy. That affects responsibility and clarity. As for commitment, coaching helps there, too, because the style's implicit message is, "I believe in you, I'm investing in you, and I expect your best efforts." Employees very often rise to that challenge with their heart, mind, and soul.

The coaching style works well in many business situations, but it is perhaps most effective when people on the receiving end are "up for it." For instance, the coaching style works particularly well when employees are already aware of their weaknesses and would like to improve their performance. Similarly, the style works well when employees realize how cultivating new abilities can help them advance. In short, it works best with employees who want to be coached.

By contrast, the coaching style makes little sense when employees, for whatever reason, are resistant to learning or changing their ways. And it flops if the leader lacks the expertise to help the employee along. The fact is, many managers are unfamiliar with or simply inept at coaching, particularly when it comes to giving ongoing performance feedback that motivates rather than creates fear or apathy. Some companies have realized the positive impact of the style and are trying to make it a core competence. At some companies, a significant portion of annual bonuses are tied to an executive's development of his or her direct reports. But many organizations have yet to take full advantage of this leadership style. Although the coaching style may not scream "bottom-line results," it delivers them.

Leaders Need Many Styles

Many studies, including this one, have shown that the more styles a leader exhibits, the better. Leaders who have mastered four or more—especially the authoritative, democratic, affiliative, and coaching styles—have the very best climate and business performance. And the most effective leaders switch flexibly among the leadership styles as needed. Although that may sound daunting, we witnessed it more often than you might guess, at both large corporations and tiny startups, by seasoned veterans who could explain exactly how and why they lead and by entrepreneurs who claim to lead by gut alone.

Such leaders don't mechanically match their style to fit a checklist of situations—they are far more fluid. They are exquisitely sensitive to the impact they are having on others and seamlessly adjust their style to get the best results. These are leaders, for example, who can read in the first minutes of conversation that a talented but under-performing employee has been demoralized by an unsympathetic, do-it-the-way-I-tell-you manager and needs to be inspired through a reminder of why her work matters. Or that leader might choose to reenergize the employee by asking her about her dreams and aspirations and finding ways to make her job more challenging. Or that initial conversation might signal that the employee needs an ultimatum: improve or leave.

For an example of fluid leadership in action, consider Joan, the general manager of a major division at a global food and beverage company. Joan was appointed to her job while the division was in a deep crisis. It had not made its profit targets for six years; in the most recent year, it had missed by $50 million. Morale among the top management team was miserable; mistrust and resentments were rampant. Joan's directive from above was clear: Turn the division around.

Joan did so with a nimbleness in switching among leadership styles that is rare. From the start, she realized she had a short window to demonstrate effective leadership and to establish rapport and trust. She also knew that she urgently needed to be informed about what was not working, so her first task was to listen to key people.

Her first week on the job she had lunch and dinner meetings with each member of the management team. Joan sought to get each person's understanding of the current situation. But her focus was not so much on learning how each person diagnosed the problem as on getting to know each manager as a person. Here Joan employed the affiliative style: She explored their lives, dreams, and aspirations.

She also stepped into the coaching role, looking for ways she could help the team members achieve what they wanted in their careers. For instance, one manager who had been getting feedback that he was a poor team player confided his worries to her. He thought he was a good team member, but he was plagued by persistent complaints. Recognizing that he was a talented executive and a valuable asset to the company, Joan made an agreement with him to point out (in private) when his actions undermined his goal of being seen as a team player.

She followed the one-on-one conversations with a three-day off-site meeting. Her goal here was team building, so that everyone would own whatever solution for the business problems emerged. Her initial stance at the off-site meeting was that of a democratic leader. She encouraged everyone to express freely their frustrations and complaints.

The next day, Joan had the group focus on solutions: Each person made three specific proposals about what needed to be done. As Joan clustered the suggestions, a natural consensus emerged about priorities for the business, such as cutting costs. As the group came up with specific action plans, Joan got the commitment and buy-in she sought.

With that vision in place, Joan shifted into the authoritative style, assigning accountability for each follow-up step to specific executives and holding them responsible for their accomplishment. For example, the division had been dropping prices on products without increasing its volume. One obvious solution was to raise prices, but the previous VP of sales had dithered and had let the problem fester. The new VP of sales now had responsibility to adjust the price points to fix the problem.

Over the following months, Joan's main stance was authoritative. She continually articulated the group's new vision in a way that reminded each member of how his or her role was crucial to achieving these goals. And, especially during the first few weeks of the plan's implementation, Joan felt that the urgency of the business crisis justified an occasional shift into the coercive style should someone fail to meet his or her responsibility. As she put it, "I had to be brutal about this follow-up and make sure this stuff happened. It was going to take discipline and focus."

The results? Every aspect of climate improved. People were innovating. They were talking about the division's vision and crowing about their commitment to new, clear goals. The ultimate proof of Joan's fluid leadership style is written in black ink: After only seven months, her division exceeded its yearly profit target by $5 million.

Growing Your Emotional Intelligence

UNLIKE IQ, which is largely genetic—it changes little from childhood—the skills of emotional intelligence can be learned at any age. It's not easy, however. Growing your emotional intelligence takes practice and commitment. But the payoffs are well worth the investment.

Consider the case of a marketing director for a division of a global food company. Jack, as I'll call him, was a classic pacesetter: high-energy, always striving to find better ways to get things done, and too eager to step in and take over when, say, someone seemed about to miss a deadline. Worse, Jack was prone to pounce on anyone who didn't seem to meet his standards, flying off the handle if a person merely deviated from completing a job in the order Jack thought best.

Jack's leadership style had a predictably disastrous impact on climate and business results. After two years of stagnant performance, Jack's boss suggested he seek out a coach. Jack wasn't pleased but, realizing his own job was on the line, he complied.

The coach, an expert in teaching people how to increase their emotional intelligence, began with a 360-degree evaluation of Jack. A diagnosis from multiple viewpoints is essential in improving emotional intelligence because those who need the most help usually have blind spots. In fact, our research found that top-performing leaders overestimate their strengths on, at most, one emotional intelligence ability, whereas poor performers overrate themselves on four or more. Jack was not that far off, but he did rate himself more glowingly than his direct reports, who gave him especially low grades on emotional self-control and empathy.

Initially, Jack had some trouble accepting the feedback data. But when his coach showed him how those weaknesses were tied to his inability to display leadership styles dependent on those competencies—especially the authoritative, affiliative, and coaching styles—Jack realized he had to improve if he wanted to advance in the company. Making such a connection is essential. The reason: Improving emotional intelligence isn't done in a weekend or during a seminar—it takes diligent practice on the job, over several months. If people do not see the value of the change, they will not make that effort.

Once Jack zeroed in on areas for improvement and committed himself to making the effort, he and his coach worked up a plan to turn his day-to-day job into a learning laboratory. For instance, Jack discovered he was empathetic when things were calm, but in a crisis, he tuned out others. This tendency hampered his ability to listen to what people were telling him in the very moments he most needed to do so. Jack's plan required him to focus on his behavior during tough situations. As soon as he felt himself tensing up, his job was to immediately step back, let the other person speak, and then ask clarifying questions. The point was to not act judgmental or hostile under pressure.

The change didn't come easily, but with practice Jack learned to defuse his flare-ups by entering into a dialogue instead of launching a harangue. Although he didn't always agree with them, at least he gave people a chance to make their case. At the same time, Jack also practiced giving his direct reports more positive feedback and reminding them of how their work contributed to the group's mission. And he restrained himself from micromanaging them.

Jack met with his coach every week or two to review his progress and get advice on specific problems. For instance, occasionally Jack would find himself falling back on his old pacesetting tactics—cutting people off, jumping in to take over, and blowing up in a rage. Almost immediately, he would regret it. So he and his coach dissected those relapses to figure out what triggered the old ways and what to do the next time a similar moment arose. Such "relapse prevention" measures inoculate people against future lapses or just giving up. Over a six-month period, Jack made real improvement. His own records showed he had reduced the number of flare-ups from one or more a day at the beginning to just one or two a month. The climate had improved sharply, and the division's numbers were starting to creep upward.

Why does improving an emotional intelligence competence take months rather than days? Because the emotional centers of the brain, not just the neocortex, are involved. The neocortex, the thinking brain that learns technical skills and purely cognitive abilities, gains knowledge very quickly, but the emotional brain does not. To master a new behavior, the emotional centers need repetition and practice. Improving your emotional intelligence, then, is akin to changing your habits. Brain circuits that carry leadership habits have to unlearn the old ones and replace them with the new. The more often a behavioral sequence is repeated, the stronger the underlying brain circuits become. At some point, the new neural pathways become the brain's default option. When that happened, Jack was able to go through the paces of leadership effortlessly, using styles that worked for him—and the whole company.

Expanding Your Repertory

Few leaders, of course, have all six styles in their repertory, and even fewer know when and how to use them. In fact, as we have brought the findings of our research into many organizations, the most common responses have been "But I have only two of those!" and "I can't use all those styles. It wouldn't be natural."

Such feelings are understandable, and in some cases, the antidote is relatively simple. The leader can build a team with members who employ styles she lacks. Take the case of a VP for manufacturing. She successfully ran a global factory system largely by using the affiliative style. She was on the road constantly, meeting with plant managers, attending to their pressing concerns, and letting them know how much she cared about them personally. She left the division's strategy—extreme efficiency—to a trusted lieutenant with a keen understanding of technology, and she delegated its performance standards to a colleague who was adept at the authoritative approach. She also had a pacesetter on her team who always visited the plants with her.

An alternative approach, and one I would recommend more, is for leaders to expand their own style repertories. To do so, leaders must first understand which emotional intelligence competencies underlie the leadership styles they are lacking. They can then work assiduously to increase their quotient of them.

For instance, an affiliative leader has strengths in three emotional intelligence competencies: in empathy, in building relationships, and in communication. Empathy—sensing how people are feeling in the moment—allows the affiliative leader to respond to employees in a way that is highly congruent with that person's emotions, thus building rapport. The affiliative leader also displays a natural ease in forming new relationships, getting to know someone as a person, and cultivating a bond. Finally, the outstanding affiliative leader has mastered the art of interpersonal communication, particularly in saying just the right thing or making the apt symbolic gesture at just the right moment.

So if you are primarily a pacesetting leader who wants to be able to use the affiliative style more often, you would need to improve your level of empathy and, perhaps, your skills at building relationships or communicating effectively. As another example, an authoritative leader who wants to add the democratic style to his repertory might need to work on the capabilities of collaboration and communication. Such advice about adding capabilities may seem simplistic—"Go change yourself"—but enhancing emotional intelligence is entirely possible with practice. (For more on how to improve emotional intelligence, see the sidebar "Growing Your Emotional Intelligence.")

More Science, Less Art

Like parenthood, leadership will never be an exact science. But neither should it be a complete mystery to those who practice it. In recent years, research has helped parents understand the genetic, psychological, and behavioral components that affect their "job performance." With our new research, leaders, too, can get a clearer picture of what it takes to lead effectively. And perhaps as important, they can see how they can make that happen.

The business environment is continually changing, and a leader must respond in kind. Hour to hour, day to day, week to week, executives must play their leadership styles like a pro—using the right one at just the right time and in the right measure. The payoff is in the results.

Originally published in March 2000. Reprint R00204

Notes

1. Daniel Goleman consults with Hay/McBer on leadership development.

The Hidden Traps in Decision-Making

by John S. Hammond, Ralph L. Keeney, and Howard Raiffa

MAKING DECISIONS IS THE MOST important job of any executive. It's also the toughest and the riskiest. Bad decisions can damage a business and a career, sometimes irreparably. So where do bad decisions come from? In many cases, they can be traced back to the way the decisions were made—the alternatives were not clearly defined, the right information was not collected, the costs and benefits were not accurately weighed. But sometimes the fault lies not in the decision-making process but rather in the mind of the decision-maker. The way the human brain works can sabotage our decisions.

Researchers have been studying the way our minds function in making decisions for half a century. This research, in the laboratory and in the field, has revealed that we use unconscious routines to cope with the complexity inherent in most decisions. These routines, known as *heuristics*, serve us well in most situations. In judging distance, for example, our minds frequently rely on a heuristic that equates clarity with proximity. The clearer an object appears, the closer we judge it to be. The fuzzier it appears, the farther away we assume it must be. This simple mental shortcut helps us to make the continuous stream of distance judgments required to navigate the world.

Yet, like most heuristics, it is not foolproof. On days that are hazier than normal, our eyes will tend to trick our minds into thinking that things are more distant than they actually are. Because the resulting distortion poses few dangers for most of us, we can safely ignore it. For airline pilots, though, the distortion can be catastrophic. That's why pilots are trained to use objective measures of distance in addition to their vision.

Researchers have identified a whole series of such flaws in the way we think in making decisions. Some, like the heuristic for clarity, are sensory misperceptions. Others take the form of biases. Others appear simply as irrational anomalies in our thinking. What makes all these traps so dangerous is their invisibility. Because they are hardwired into our thinking process, we fail to recognize them—even as we fall right into them.

For executives, whose success hinges on the many day-to-day decisions they make or approve, the psychological traps are especially dangerous. They can undermine everything from new-product development to acquisition and divestiture strategy to succession planning. While no one can rid his or her mind of these ingrained flaws, anyone can follow the lead of airline pilots and learn to understand the traps and compensate for them.

In this article, we examine a number of well-documented psychological traps that are particularly likely to undermine business decisions. In addition to reviewing the causes and manifestations of these traps, we offer some specific ways managers can guard against them. It's important to remember, though, that the best defense is always awareness. Executives who attempt to familiarize themselves with these traps and the diverse forms they take will be better able to ensure that the decisions they make are sound and that the recommendations proposed by subordinates or associates are reliable.

The Anchoring Trap

How would you answer these two questions?

- Is the population of Turkey greater than 35 million?

- What's your best estimate of Turkey's population?

Idea in Brief

Bad decisions can often be traced back to the way the decisions were made—the alternatives were not clearly defined, the right information was not collected, the costs and benefits were not accurately weighed. But sometimes the fault lies not in the decision-making process but rather in the mind of the decision-maker: The way the human brain works can sabotage the choices we make. In this article, first published in 1998, John S. Hammond, Ralph L. Keeney, and Howard Raiffa examine eight psychological traps that can affect the way we make business decisions. The anchoring trap leads us to give disproportionate weight to the first information we receive. The status-quo trap biases us toward maintaining the current situation—even when better alternatives exist. The sunk-cost trap inclines us to perpetuate

the mistakes of the past. The confirming-evidence trap leads us to seek out information supporting an existing predilection and to discount opposing information. The framing trap occurs when we misstate a problem, undermining the entire decision-making process. The overconfidence trap makes us overestimate the accuracy of our forecasts. The prudence trap leads us to be overcautious when we make estimates about uncertain events. And the recallability trap prompts us to give undue weight to recent, dramatic events. The best way to avoid all the traps is awareness: Forewarned is forearmed. But executives can also take other simple steps to protect themselves and their organizations from these mental lapses to ensure that their important business decisions are sound and reliable.

If you're like most people, the figure of 35 million cited in the first question (a figure we chose arbitrarily) influenced your answer to the second question. Over the years, we've posed those questions to many groups of people. In half the cases, we used 35 million in the first question; in the other half, we used 100 million. Without fail, the answers to the second question increase by many millions when the larger figure is used in the first question. This simple test illustrates the common and often pernicious mental phenomenon known as *anchoring*. When considering a decision, the mind gives disproportionate weight to the first information it receives. Initial impressions, estimates, or data anchor subsequent thoughts and judgments.

Anchors take many guises. They can be as simple and seemingly innocuous as a comment offered by a colleague or a statistic appearing in the morning newspaper. They can be as insidious as a stereotype about a person's skin color, accent, or dress. In business, one of the most common types of anchors is a past event or trend. A marketer attempting to project the sales of a product for the coming year often begins by looking at the sales volumes for past years. The old numbers become anchors, which the forecaster then adjusts based on other factors. This approach, while it may lead to a reasonably accurate estimate, tends to give too much weight to past events and not enough weight to other factors. In situations characterized by rapid changes in the marketplace, historical anchors can lead to poor forecasts and, in turn, misguided choices.

Because anchors can establish the terms on which a decision will be made, they are often used as a bargaining tactic by savvy negotiators. Consider the experience of a large consulting firm that was searching for new office space in San Francisco. Working with a commercial real-estate broker, the firm's partners identified a building that met all their criteria, and they set up a meeting with the building's owners. The owners opened the meeting by laying out the terms of a proposed contract: a 10-year lease; an initial monthly price of $2.50 per square foot; annual price increases at the prevailing inflation rate; all interior improvements to be the tenant's responsibility; an option for the tenant to extend the lease for 10 additional years under the same terms. Although the price was at the high end of current market rates, the consultants made a relatively modest counteroffer. They proposed an initial price in the midrange of market rates and asked the owners to share in the renovation expenses, but they accepted all the other terms. The consultants could have been much more aggressive and creative in their counterproposal—reducing the initial price to the low end of market rates, adjusting rates biennially rather than annually, putting a cap on the increases, defining different terms for extending the lease, and so forth—but their thinking was guided by the owners' initial proposal. The consultants had fallen into the anchoring trap, and as a result, they ended up paying a lot more for the space than they had to.

What can you do about it?

The effect of anchors in decision-making has been documented in thousands of experiments. Anchors influence the decisions not only of managers but also of accountants and engineers, bankers and lawyers, consultants and stock analysts. No one can avoid their influence; they're just too widespread. But managers who are aware of the dangers of anchors can reduce their impact by using the following techniques:

- Always view a problem from different perspectives. Try using alternative starting points and approaches rather than sticking with the first line of thought that occurs to you.

- Think about the problem on your own before consulting others to avoid becoming anchored by their ideas.

- Be open-minded. Seek information and opinions from a variety of people to widen your frame of reference and to push your mind in fresh directions.

- Be careful to avoid anchoring your advisers, consultants, and others from whom you solicit information and counsel. Tell them as little as possible about your own ideas, estimates, and tentative decisions. If you reveal too much, your own preconceptions may simply come back to you.

- Be particularly wary of anchors in negotiations. Think through your position before any negotiation begins in order to avoid being anchored by the other party's initial proposal. At the same time, look for opportunities to use anchors to your own advantage—if you're the seller, for example, suggest a high, but defensible, price as an opening gambit.

The Status-Quo Trap

We all like to believe that we make decisions rationally and objectively. But the fact is, we all carry biases, and those biases influence the choices we make. Decision-makers display, for example, a strong bias toward alternatives that perpetuate the status quo. On a broad scale, we can see this tendency whenever a radically new product is introduced. The first automobiles, revealingly called "horseless carriages," looked very much like the buggies they replaced. The first "electronic newspapers" appearing on the World Wide Web looked very much like their print precursors.

On a more familiar level, you may have succumbed to this bias in your personal financial decisions. People sometimes, for example, inherit shares of stock that they would never have bought themselves. Although it would be a straightforward, inexpensive proposition to sell those shares and put the money into a different investment, a surprising number of people don't sell. They find the status quo comfortable, and they avoid taking action that would upset it. "Maybe I'll rethink it later," they say. But "later" is usually never.

The source of the status-quo trap lies deep within our psyches, in our desire to protect our egos from damage. Breaking from the status quo means taking action, and when we take action, we take responsibility, thus opening ourselves to criticism and to regret. Not surprisingly, we naturally look for reasons to do nothing. Sticking with the status quo represents, in most cases, the safer course because it puts us at less psychological risk.

Many experiments have shown the magnetic attraction of the status quo. In one, a group of people were randomly given one of two gifts of approximately the same value—half received a mug, the other half a Swiss chocolate bar. They were then told that they could easily exchange the gift they received for the other gift. While you might expect that about half would have wanted to make the exchange, only one in 10 actually did. The status quo exerted its power even though it had been arbitrarily established only minutes before.

Other experiments have shown that the more choices you are given, the more pull the status quo has. More people will, for instance, choose the status quo when there are two alternatives to it rather than one: A and B instead of just A. Why? Choosing between A and B requires additional effort; selecting the status quo avoids that effort.

In business, where sins of commission (doing something) tend to be punished much more severely than sins of omission (doing nothing), the status quo holds a particularly strong attraction. Many mergers, for example, founder because the acquiring company avoids taking swift action to impose a new, more appropriate management structure on the acquired company. "Let's not rock the boat right now," the typical reasoning goes. "Let's wait until the situation stabilizes." But as time passes, the existing structure becomes more entrenched, and altering it becomes harder, not easier. Having failed to seize the occasion when change would have been expected, management finds itself stuck with the status quo.

What can you do about it?
First of all, remember that in any given decision, maintaining the status quo may indeed be the best choice, but you don't want to choose it just because it is comfortable. Once you become aware of the status-quo trap, you can use these techniques to lessen its pull:

- Always remind yourself of your objectives and examine how they would be served by the status quo. You may find that elements of the current situation act as barriers to your goals.

- Never think of the status quo as your only alternative. Identify other options and use them as counterbalances, carefully evaluating all the pluses and minuses.

- Ask yourself whether you would choose the status-quo alternative if, in fact, it weren't the status quo.

- Avoid exaggerating the effort or cost involved in switching from the status quo.

- Remember that the desirability of the status quo will change over time. When comparing alternatives, always evaluate them in terms of the future as well as the present.

- If you have several alternatives that are superior to the status quo, don't default to the status quo just because you're having a hard time picking the best alternative. Force yourself to choose.

The Sunk-Cost Trap

Another of our deep-seated biases is to make choices in a way that justifies past choices, even when the past choices no longer seem valid. Most of us have fallen into this trap. We may have refused, for example, to sell a stock or a mutual fund at a loss, forgoing other, more attractive investments. Or we may have poured enormous effort into improving the performance of an employee whom we knew we shouldn't have hired in the first place. Our past decisions become what economists term *sunk costs*—old investments of time or money that are now irrecoverable. We know, rationally, that sunk costs are irrelevant to the present decision, but nevertheless they prey on our minds, leading us to make inappropriate decisions.

Why can't people free themselves from past decisions? Frequently, it's because they are unwilling, consciously or not, to admit to a mistake. Acknowledging a poor decision in one's personal life may be purely a private matter, involving only one's self-esteem, but in business, a bad decision is often a very public matter, inviting critical comments from colleagues or bosses. If you fire a poor performer whom you hired, you're making a public admission of poor judgment. It seems psychologically safer to let him or her stay on, even though that choice only compounds the error.

The sunk-cost bias shows up with disturbing regularity in banking, where it can have particularly dire consequences. When a borrower's business runs into trouble, a lender will often advance additional funds in hopes of providing the business with some breathing room to recover. If the business does have a good chance of coming back, that's a wise investment. Otherwise, it's just throwing good money after bad.

One of us helped a major U.S. bank recover after it made many bad loans to foreign businesses. We found that the bankers responsible for originating the problem loans were far more likely to advance additional funds—repeatedly, in many cases—than were bankers who took over the accounts after the original loans were made. Too often, the original bankers' strategy—and loans—ended in failure. Having been trapped by an escalation of commitment, they had tried, consciously or unconsciously, to protect their earlier, flawed decisions. They had fallen victim to the sunk-cost bias. The bank finally solved the problem by instituting a policy requiring that a loan be immediately reassigned to another banker as soon as any problem arose. The new banker was able to take a fresh, unbiased look at the merit of offering more funds.

Sometimes a corporate culture reinforces the sunk-cost trap. If the penalties for making a decision that leads to an unfavorable outcome are overly severe, managers will be motivated to let failed projects drag on endlessly—in the vain hope that they'll somehow be able to transform them into successes. Executives should recognize that, in an uncertain world where unforeseeable events are common, good decisions can sometimes lead to bad outcomes. By acknowledging that some good ideas will end in failure, executives will encourage people to cut their losses rather than let them mount.

What can you do about it?
For all decisions with a history, you will need to make a conscious effort to set aside any sunk costs—whether psychological or economic—that will muddy your thinking about the choice at hand. Try these techniques:

- Seek out and listen carefully to the views of people who were uninvolved with the earlier decisions and who are hence unlikely to be committed to them.

- Examine why admitting to an earlier mistake distresses you. If the problem lies in your own wounded self-esteem, deal with it head-on. Remind yourself that even smart choices can have bad consequences, through no fault of the original decision-maker, and that even the best and most experienced managers are not immune to errors in judgment. Remember the wise words of Warren Buffett: "When you find yourself in a hole, the best thing you can do is stop digging."

- Be on the lookout for the influence of sunk-cost biases in the decisions and recommendations made by your subordinates. Reassign responsibilities when necessary.

- Don't cultivate a failure-fearing culture that leads employees to perpetuate their mistakes. In rewarding people, look at the quality of their decision-making (taking into account what was known at the time their decisions were made), not just the quality of the outcomes.

The Confirming-Evidence Trap

Imagine that you're the president of a successful midsize U.S. manufacturer considering whether to call off a planned plant expansion. For a while you've been concerned that your company won't be able to sustain the rapid pace of growth of its exports. You fear that the value of the U.S. dollar will strengthen in coming months, making your goods more costly for overseas consumers and dampening demand. But before you put the brakes on the plant expansion, you decide to call up an acquaintance, the chief executive of a similar company that recently mothballed a new factory, to check her reasoning. She presents a strong case that other currencies are about to weaken significantly against the dollar. What do you do?

You'd better not let that conversation be the clincher, because you've probably just fallen victim to the confirming-evidence bias. This bias leads us to seek out information that supports our existing instinct or point of view while avoiding information that contradicts it. What, after all, did you expect your acquaintance to give, other than a strong argument in favor of her own decision? The confirming-evidence bias not only affects where we go to collect evidence but also how we interpret the evidence we do receive, leading us to give too much weight to supporting information and too little to conflicting information.

In one psychological study of this phenomenon, two groups—one opposed to and one supporting capital punishment—each read two reports of carefully conducted research on the effectiveness of the death penalty as a deterrent to crime. One report concluded that the death penalty was effective; the other concluded it was not. Despite being exposed to solid scientific information supporting counterarguments, the members of both groups became even more convinced of the validity of their own position after reading both reports. They automatically accepted the supporting information and dismissed the conflicting information.

There are two fundamental psychological forces at work here. The first is our tendency to subconsciously decide what we want to do before we figure out why we want to do it. The second is our inclination to be more engaged by things we like than by things we dislike—a tendency well-documented even in babies. Naturally, then, we are drawn to information that supports our subconscious leanings.

What can you do about it?

It's not that you shouldn't make the choice you're subconsciously drawn to. It's just that you want to be sure it's the smart choice. You need to put it to the test. Here's how:

- Always check to see whether you are examining all the evidence with equal rigor. Avoid the tendency to accept confirming evidence without question.

- Get someone you respect to play devil's advocate, to argue against the decision you're contemplating. Better yet, build the counterarguments yourself. What's the strongest reason to do something else? The second strongest reason? The third? Consider the position with an open mind.

- Be honest with yourself about your motives. Are you really gathering information to help you make a smart choice, or are you just looking for evidence confirming what you think you'd like to do?

- In seeking the advice of others, don't ask leading questions that invite confirming evidence. And if you find that an adviser always seems to support your point of view, find a new adviser. Don't surround yourself with yes-men.

The Framing Trap

The first step in making a decision is to frame the question. It's also one of the most dangerous steps. The way a problem is framed can profoundly influence the choices you make. In a case involving automobile insurance, for example, framing made a $200 million difference. To reduce insurance costs, two neighboring states, New Jersey and Pennsylvania, made similar changes in their laws. Each state gave drivers a new option: By accepting a limited right to sue, they could lower their premiums. But the two states framed the choice in very different ways: In New Jersey, you automatically got the limited right to sue unless you specified otherwise; in Pennsylvania, you got the full right to sue unless you specified otherwise. The different frames established different status quos, and, not surprisingly, most consumers defaulted to the status quo. As a result, in New Jersey about 80% of drivers chose the limited right to sue, but in Pennsylvania only 25% chose it. Because of the way it framed the choice, Pennsylvania failed to gain approximately $200 million in expected insurance and litigation savings.

The framing trap can take many forms, and as the insurance example shows, it is often closely related to other psychological traps. A frame can establish the status quo or introduce an anchor. It can highlight sunk costs or lead you toward confirming evidence. Decision researchers have documented two types of frames that distort decision-making with particular frequency.

Frames as gains versus losses

In a study patterned after a classic experiment by decision researchers Daniel Kahneman and Amos Tversky, one of us posed the following problem to a group of insurance professionals:

> You are a marine property adjuster charged with minimizing the loss of cargo on three insured barges that sank yesterday off the coast of Alaska. Each barge holds $200,000 worth of cargo, which will be lost if not salvaged within 72 hours. The owner of a local marine-salvage company gives you two options, both of which will cost the same:
>
> *Plan A:* This plan will save the cargo of one of the three barges, worth $200,000.
>
> *Plan B:* This plan has a one-third probability of saving the cargo on all three barges, worth $600,000, but has a two-thirds probability of saving nothing.
>
> Which plan would you choose?

If you are like 71% of the respondents in the study, you chose the "less risky" Plan A, which will save one barge for sure. Another group in the study, however, was asked to choose between alternatives C and D:

Plan C: This plan will result in the loss of two of the three cargoes, worth $400,000.

Plan D: This plan has a two-thirds probability of resulting in the loss of all three cargoes and the entire $600,000 but has a one-third probability of losing no cargo.

Faced with this choice, 80% of these respondents preferred Plan D. The pairs of alternatives are, of course, precisely equivalent—Plan A is the same as Plan C, and Plan B is the same as Plan D—they've just been framed in different ways. The strikingly different responses reveal that people are risk averse when a problem is posed in terms of gains (barges saved) but risk seeking when a problem is posed in terms of avoiding losses (barges lost). Furthermore, they tend to adopt the frame as it is presented to them rather than restating the problem in their own way.

Framing with different reference points

The same problem can also elicit very different responses when frames use different reference points. Let's say you have $2,000 in your checking account and you are asked the following question:

Would you accept a 50/50 chance of either losing $300 or winning $500?

Would you accept the chance? What if you were asked this question:

Would you prefer to keep your checking account balance of $2,000 or to accept a 50/50 chance of having either $1,700 or $2,500 in your account?

Once again, the two questions pose the same problem. While your answers to both questions should, rationally speaking, be the same, studies have shown that many people would refuse the 50/50 chance in the first question but accept it in the second. Their different reactions result from the different reference points presented in the two frames. The first frame, with its reference point of zero, emphasizes incremental gains and losses, and the thought of losing triggers a conservative response in many people's minds. The second frame, with its reference point of $2,000, puts things into perspective by emphasizing the real financial impact of the decision.

What can you do about it?
A poorly framed problem can undermine even the best-considered decision. But any adverse effect of framing can be limited by taking the following precautions:

- Don't automatically accept the initial frame, whether it was formulated by you or by someone else. Always try to reframe the problem in various ways. Look for distortions caused by the frames.

- Try posing problems in a neutral, redundant way that combines gains and losses or embraces different reference points. For example: Would you accept a 50/50 chance of either losing $300, resulting in a bank balance of $1,700, or winning $500, resulting in a bank balance of $2,500?

- Think hard throughout your decision-making process about the framing of the problem. At points throughout the process, particularly near the end, ask yourself how your thinking might change if the framing changed.

- When others recommend decisions, examine the way they framed the problem. Challenge them with different frames.

The Estimating and Forecasting Traps

Most of us are adept at making estimates about time, distance, weight, and volume. That's because we're constantly making judgments about these variables and getting quick feedback about the accuracy of those judgments. Through daily practice, our minds become finely calibrated.

Making estimates or forecasts about uncertain events, however, is a different matter. While managers continually make such estimates and forecasts, they rarely get clear feedback about their accuracy. If you judge, for example, that the likelihood of the price of oil falling to less than $15 a barrel one year hence is about 40% and the price does indeed fall to that level, you can't tell whether you were right or wrong about the probability you estimated. The only way to gauge your accuracy would be to keep track of many, many similar judgments to see if, after the fact, the events you thought had a 40% chance of occurring actually did occur 40% of the time. That would require a great deal of data, carefully tracked over a long period of time. Weather forecasters and bookmakers have the opportunities and incentives to maintain such records, but the rest of us don't. As a result, our minds never become calibrated for making estimates in the face of uncertainty.

All of the traps we've discussed so far can influence the way we make decisions when confronted with uncertainty. But there's another set of traps that can have a particularly distorting effect in uncertain situations because they cloud our ability to assess probabilities. Let's look at three of the most common of these uncertainty traps.

The overconfidence trap

Even though most of us are not very good at making estimates or forecasts, we actually tend to be overconfident about our accuracy. That can lead to errors in judgment and, in turn, bad decisions. In one series of tests, people were asked to forecast the next week's closing value for the Dow Jones Industrial Average. To account for uncertainty, they were then asked to estimate a range within which the closing value would likely fall. In picking the top number of the range, they were asked to choose a high estimate they thought had only a 1% chance of being exceeded by the closing value. Similarly, for the bottom end, they were told to pick a low estimate for which they thought there would be only a 1% chance of the closing value falling below it. If they were good at judging their forecasting accuracy, you'd expect the participants to be wrong only about 2% of the time. But hundreds of tests have shown that the actual Dow Jones averages fell outside the forecast ranges 20% to 30% of the time. Overly confident about the accuracy of their predictions, most people set too narrow a range of possibilities.

Think of the implications for business decisions, in which major initiatives and investments often hinge on ranges of estimates. If managers underestimate the high end or overestimate the low end of a crucial variable, they may miss attractive opportunities or expose themselves to far greater risk than they realize. Much money has been wasted on ill-fated product-development projects because managers did not accurately account for the possibility of market failure.

The prudence trap

Another trap for forecasters takes the form of overcautiousness, or prudence. When faced with high-stakes decisions, we tend to adjust our estimates or forecasts "just to be on the safe side." Many years ago, for example, one of the Big Three U.S. automakers was deciding how many of a new-model car to produce in anticipation of its busiest sales season. The market-planning department, responsible for the decision, asked other departments to supply forecasts of key variables such as anticipated sales, dealer inventories, competitor actions, and costs. Knowing the purpose of the estimates, each department slanted its forecast to favor building more cars—"just to be safe." But the market planners took the numbers at face value and then made their own "just to be safe" adjustments. Not surprisingly, the number of cars produced far exceeded demand, and the company took six months to sell off the surplus, resorting in the end to promotional pricing.

Policy makers have gone so far as to codify overcautiousness in formal decision procedures. An extreme example is the methodology of "worst-case analysis," which was once popular in the design of weapons systems and is still used in certain engineering and regulatory settings. Using this approach, engineers designed weapons to operate under the worst possible combination of circumstances, even though the odds of those circumstances actually coming to pass were infinitesimal. Worst-case analysis added enormous costs with no practical benefit (in fact, it often backfired by touching off an arms race), proving that too much prudence can sometimes be as dangerous as too little.

The recallability trap

Even if we are neither overly confident nor unduly prudent, we can still fall into a trap when making estimates or forecasts. Because we frequently base our predictions about future events on our memory of past events, we can be overly influenced by dramatic events—those that leave a strong impression on our memory. We all, for example, exaggerate the probability of rare but catastrophic occurrences such as plane crashes because they get disproportionate attention in the media. A dramatic or traumatic event in your own life can also distort your thinking. You will assign a higher probability to traffic accidents if you have passed one on the way to work, and you will assign a higher chance of someday dying of cancer yourself if a close friend has died of the disease.

In fact, anything that distorts your ability to recall events in a balanced way will distort your probability assessments. In one experiment, lists of well-known men and women were read to different groups of people. Unbeknownst to the subjects, each list had an equal number of men and women, but on some lists the men were more famous than the women while on others the women were more famous. Afterward, the participants were asked to estimate the percentages of men and women on each list. Those who had heard the list with the more famous men thought there were more men on the list, while those who had heard the one with the more famous women thought there were more women.

Corporate lawyers often get caught in the recallability trap when defending liability suits. Their decisions about whether to settle a claim or take it to court usually hinge on their assessments of the possible outcomes of a trial. Because the media tends to aggressively publicize massive damage awards (while ignoring other, far more common trial outcomes), lawyers can overestimate the probability of a large award for the plaintiff. As a result, they offer larger settlements than are actually warranted.

What can you do about it?
The best way to avoid the estimating and forecasting traps is to take a very disciplined approach to making forecasts and judging probabilities. For each of the three traps, some additional precautions can be taken:

- To reduce the effects of overconfidence in making estimates, always start by considering the extremes, the low and high ends of the possible range of values. This will help you avoid being anchored by an initial estimate. Then challenge your estimates of the extremes. Try to imagine circumstances where the actual figure would fall below your low or above your high, and adjust your range accordingly. Challenge the estimates of your subordinates and advisers in a similar fashion. They're also susceptible to overconfidence.

- To avoid the prudence trap, always state your estimates honestly and explain to anyone who will be using them that they have not been adjusted. Emphasize the need for honest input to anyone who will be supplying you with estimates. Test estimates over a reasonable range to assess their impact. Take a second look at the more sensitive estimates.

- To minimize the distortion caused by variations in recallability, carefully examine all your assumptions to ensure they're not unduly influenced by your memory. Get actual statistics whenever possible. Try not to be guided by impressions.

Forewarned Is Forearmed

When it comes to business decisions, there's rarely such a thing as a no-brainer. Our brains are always at work, sometimes, unfortunately, in ways that hinder rather than help us. At every stage of the decision-making process, misperceptions, biases, and other tricks of the mind can influence the choices we make. Highly complex and important decisions are the most prone to distortion because they tend to involve the most assumptions, the most estimates, and the most inputs from the most people. The higher the stakes, the higher the risk of being caught in a psychological trap.

The traps we've reviewed can all work in isolation. But, even more dangerous, they can work in concert, amplifying one another. A dramatic first impression might anchor our thinking, and then we might selectively seek out confirming evidence to justify our initial inclination. We make a hasty decision, and that decision establishes a new status quo. As our sunk costs mount, we become trapped, unable to find a propitious time to seek out a new and possibly better course. The psychological miscues cascade, making it harder and harder to choose wisely.

As we said at the outset, the best protection against all psychological traps—in isolation or in combination—is awareness. Forewarned is forearmed. Even if you can't eradicate the distortions ingrained into the way your mind works, you can build tests and disciplines into your decision-making process that can uncover errors in thinking before they become errors in judgment. And taking action to understand and avoid psychological traps can have the added benefit of increasing your confidence in the choices you make.

Originally published in January 2006. Reprint R0601K

Stop Wasting Valuable Time

by Michael C. Mankins

A FEW DAYS BEFORE AnyCo's biweekly top management team meeting, the CEO's assistant sends out an email asking attendees to submit agenda items. A hodgepodge of suggestions comes back. The head of HR wants to update the team on a nasty age discrimination lawsuit that's about to go to trial. The executive vice president for the European business division wants to discuss disturbing competitive trends in her region. The CIO asks for a few minutes to review plans for Sarbanes-Oxley compliance. The manager of the largest North American business unit needs to present a major capital investment proposal for a factory automation program. The marketing senior vice president has to show some alternatives for a big print-advertising campaign. And the CEO himself wants to kick off an effort to revamp the company's annual planning and budgeting process.

The assistant creates a draft agenda, listing the items in the order they were submitted, allots a best guess of the time needed for each, and runs it by the CEO. He reorders the agenda a bit, putting the routine, operational items up front to ensure that the bulk of the meeting is focused on strategic issues.

But when the meeting takes place, his plan goes awry. The group has a long, drawn-out debate about the look and feel of the advertising campaign, and the discussion of Sarbanes-Oxley turns into a gripe session about the IT department. The executives end up with little time to devote to the deeper business issues. They give the factory automation plan a green light after a cursory examination—to the CFO's great discomfort. They put off consideration of European competition for a future meeting. And they have an unfocused and ultimately inconclusive discussion about the CEO's new planning process. When the meeting breaks up—an hour late—people leave in a sour and cynical mood, complaining to themselves about another waste of valuable time.

The scenario I've just described is played out on a regular basis at almost any company you might name, including, most probably, your own. For although time is the scarcest resource in any company—after all, no amount of money can buy a 25-hour day—the sad reality is that few top executive teams manage their time at all well. As we'll see in the following pages, the typical company's senior executives spend less than three days each month working together as a team—and in that time they devote less than three *hours* to strategic issues. Moreover, in my experience, those three hours are seldom well spent: Strategy discussions tend to be diffuse and unstructured, only rarely designed to reach good decisions quickly.

The price of misused executive time is high. Apart from the frustrations that individual managers suffer, delayed or distorted strategic decisions lead to overlooked waste and high costs, hastily conceived and harmful cost reductions, missed new product and business development opportunities, and poor long-term investments.

But as I will also show, drawing on the experiences of my firm's clients, a few deceptively simple changes in the way top management teams set agendas and structure meetings can make an enormous difference in their efficiency and effectiveness. And once the members of the leadership team get the basics right, they can make more fundamental changes in the way they work together. Strategy making can be transformed from a series of fragmented and unproductive events into a streamlined, effective, and ongoing management dialogue. For companies that have done this, management meetings aren't a necessary evil; they're a source of real competitive

Idea in Brief

Most leadership teams spend just three hours per month making strategic decisions. That translates into less than a week per year. Worse, many teams fritter away those precious hours on unfocused, inconclusive discussion rather than rapid, well-informed decision-making.

The consequences? Delayed decisions that lead to wasted resources, missed opportunities, and poor long-term investments. One global firm spent more time each year selecting its holiday card than it did debating a vital Africa strategy.

How can your leadership team avoid such pitfalls? Spend your limited time on issues exerting the greatest impact on your company's long-term value. Deal with operations separately from strategy. Put real choices on the table, evaluating at least three viable options for every strategy. Use meeting time for decision-making—not just discussion—and agree on what was decided. And move issues off your agenda as quickly as possible.

Your reward? Strategic decisions—made better and faster.

advantage, enabling top executives to make better decisions and to make them faster.

How Valuable Time Is Squandered

A very real constraint on the financial performance of most companies is top management's capacity to reach good decisions quickly. Both quality and pace are important. Obviously, poor decisions made too quickly will lead to actions that destroy shareholder value. But good—even great—decisions made too slowly can depress company performance as well. Unfortunately, research shows, few companies manage executive time in a disciplined or systematic way.

In the fall of 2003, my firm, Marakon Associates, collaborated with the Economist Intelligence Unit to conduct a survey of top management team members (the CEO, COO, CFO, business unit presidents, managing directors, and so on) from 187 companies worldwide with market capitalizations of at least $1 billion. We wanted to understand how these teams invest their collective time. Specifically, we wanted to know how much time top managers spend together as a

Idea in Practice

Apply these practices to make the best use of your leadership team's time:

Deal with Strategy and Operations Separately

Holding separate meetings for each prevents day-to-day operations from dominating your team's agenda and liberates time for substantive strategy debates.

> *Example:* Dutch banking giant ABN AMRO's board used to spend only about an hour per month on strategy, with most of its meeting time devoted to day-to-day operational details. But market changes required a more strategic focus. The board now spends slightly less time together—but devotes much more of that time to strategy, typically about 10 hours per month.

Focus on Decisions, Not Discussions

Enhance the quality and pace of your team's decision-making, for example by distributing reading materials in advance of meetings. Specify why participants must read them (e.g., for information only? discussion and debate? decision-making?) This readies participants to devote precious meeting time to deciding crucial issues.

Measure the Real Value of Every Agenda Item

Prioritize meeting agenda items according to each issue's impact on your company's long-term value. Address high-value issues only, and delegate low-value issues to lower organizational levels.

> *Example:* At Roche, the Swiss drug and diagnostic product maker, CEO Franz Humer created a "decision agenda" comprising the 10 most important opportunities and problems facing the company. Leaders regularly update the agenda by quantifying the value at stake for each issue and spend over

team and, when they meet, how they set priorities, how they manage the time, and how successful they think they are at reaching important decisions.

Even though the companies surveyed compete in different geographic markets and in disparate industries—ranging from telecommunications equipment to wholesale banking to consumer foods—top managers were remarkably consistent in their views of how effective their executive team meetings are. Our findings support what many executives have long suspected—namely, that they half of their meeting time on those 10 items. This process has transformed the quality and pace of Roche's strategic decision-making.

Get Issues Off the Agenda Quickly

Develop clear timetables detailing when and how participants will decide each issue and who will approve final strategy.

Example: At Cardinal Health, a pharmaceutical and medical supply distributor, senior managers continually ask themselves, "When must this decision be made?" and ensure that they reach decisions within a predetermined time. Results? Less overanalysis and more rapid decision-making.

Put Real Choices on the Table

Evaluate at least three viable alternatives (not just minor variations on one theme) before approving any strategy. This encourages teams to choose the best course of action, not just the most obvious. By debating alternative strategies, British retail bank Lloyds TSB decided to exit international markets, helping to expand its market value 40-fold between 1983 and 2001.

Make Decisions Stick

Explicitly agree on what was decided in the meeting. Then specify the resources (time, talent, and money) required to execute the strategy, as well as the financial results you've committed to deliver.

spend too much time discussing issues that have little or no direct impact on company value. Even worse, their meetings often fail to produce both the quality and quantity of decisions required to drive superior performance. Specifically, here's what we discovered.

Top management teams spend relatively little time together
Executives at the companies we surveyed spent an average of 21 hours a month together in leadership team meetings. Moreover, the time they spent in any one meeting was relatively short, seldom

more than four hours at a stretch—and less in bigger companies whose management teams were widely dispersed geographically. Given the importance of the top team's decisions to company value, it's clearly imperative that such limited time is used wisely. Sadly, that was hardly the case.

Agenda setting is unfocused and undisciplined

At half the companies surveyed, top management's agenda was either exactly the same from meeting to meeting or ad hoc. In fact, when asked how they set meeting priorities, most executives said they were driven by the crisis of the moment ("We have a production problem in Unit A; therefore, this month we will focus top management on Unit A"); historical precedent ("Every November, we review our human resource policies"); or egalitarianism ("Everyone in the room will get his or her chance to speak").

In many companies, the problem is compounded by the fact that no one is explicitly responsible for managing the leadership team's agenda. So the process for getting important matters in front of top management can be inefficient, even sloppy. One firm in our sample, for example, set top management's agenda through what it described as a "first in, first on" process—where (as in our hypothetical example) the CEO's secretary set the agenda by adding topics as they were phoned in by executive team members. Not surprisingly, too many items frequently ended up on the agenda and, consequently, the team often ran out of time before it could address key items.

Less than 5% of survey respondents said their company had a rigorous and disciplined process for focusing top management's time on the most important issues. The results are all too predictable. The urgent crowds out the important, and meetings end late, frustrating team members, or—worse yet—end on time without reaching important decisions. In effect, top management delegates many of the company's most important issues to lower levels in the organization—to individuals ill equipped to deal with the problems' underlying complexity and poorly placed to see the larger ramifications of their decisions. Such decisions often conflict, as a strategy chosen by one unit works against the strategy chosen by another, slowing execution and undermining performance.

How to Get the Time Back

SEVEN TECHNIQUES can help you get control of your top management agenda and make sure meeting time is spent building value.

1. Deal with operations separately from strategy.
2. Focus on decisions, not on discussions.
3. Measure the real value of every item on the agenda.
4. Get issues off the agenda as quickly as possible.
5. Put real choices on the table.
6. Adopt common decision-making processes and standards.
7. Make decisions stick.

Too little attention is paid to strategy

It's probably not surprising, given the ad hoc way meeting priorities are set at most companies, that top management spends less than three hours a month discussing strategy issues (including mergers and acquisitions) or making strategic decisions. In fact, our research reveals, as much as 80% of top management's time is devoted to issues that account for less than 20% of a company's long-term value. At one global financial service firm in our survey, for example, a senior line executive reported that top executives spent more time each year selecting the company's holiday card than debating the bank's strategy for the entire continent of Africa (where they had made significant capital investments). They are hardly exceptional: The exhibit "Where the time goes" gives a detailed breakdown of how a typical top management team spends its time.

Top management meetings aren't structured to produce real decisions

Most leadership team meetings (more than 65%, according to our research) are not even called for the purpose of making a decision. They're held for "information sharing," "group input," or "group discussion." The meetings that do focus on strategy are most commonly off-site brainstorming sessions—typically amorphous events that produce few tangible outputs. As a consequence, very few executives surveyed

Where the time goes

Here's how, on average, top management teams spend their time together in any given year; only 15% is devoted to strategic issues.

Total top management time	**250 hours per year**
Minus:	
Operating performance reviews	**62 hours**
Crises of the moment	**27 hours**
Administrative issues and policy	**22 hours**
Workforce issues	**22 hours**
Corporate governance	**18 hours**
Financial policy	**14 hours**
Investor communications and guidance	**12 hours**
Team building	**11 hours**
Succession planning	**10 hours**
Litigation	**6 hours**
Community service and social responsibility	**6 hours**
Other	**3 hours**
Total nonstrategy time	**213 hours**
Time left over for:	**37 hours per year**
Strategy development and approval	**3 hours per month**

(only 12%) believed that their top management meetings consistently produced decisions on important strategic or organizational issues.

When leadership team meetings do produce decisions, many organizations have difficulty making them stick. Once the meeting ends and the team disbands, participants often take away very different interpretations of the group's decision. Some members may be unhappy that the team didn't go far enough in its decision, and they work to stretch the group's mandate as far as possible in communications down the line. Others may view the team's decision as incomplete or tentative and communicate only high-level guidance to subordinates, effectively delaying execution until management provides clearer direction. Still others may think the team's decision is inappropriate or just plain wrong. They can issue what amounts to a silent veto by relaying nothing to the troops, hindering (or even preventing) execution.

Seven Techniques for Exploiting Valuable Time

Serious as they are, the problems I have described can be fixed. At a number of companies—ABN AMRO, Alcan, Barclays, Boeing, Cadbury Schweppes, Cardinal Health, Gillette, Lloyds TSB, and Roche— executives have found ways to improve teamwork at the top. Leaders spend their time together addressing the issues that have the greatest impact on the company's long-term value. The top management team employs rigorous processes to produce high-quality decisions at pace. As a result, these firms have generated better financial performance and higher rates of value growth than their competitors.

While every executive team we studied is different and faces different challenges, we have been able to identify seven common techniques they all use in some form to manage their agendas and achieve superior value growth. To make the most of the limited time that top management spends together each year, executives at the most successful companies:

Deal with operations separately from strategy
Reviewing operating performance and making strategy decisions are distinct activities, requiring different modes of discussion and

different mindsets. Our research suggests that the most success-ful companies hold separate meetings for each purpose. This pre-vents day-to-day operations from dominating the leadership team's agenda and frees up time for substantive strategy debates. Dutch banking giant ABN AMRO has recently taken this approach as part of its new management framework.

In the early 1990s, the bank's managing board—comprising the chairman and the top five executives—spent most of its time review-ing loans and discussing day-to-day operations. That wasn't a prob-lem in those days, when ABN AMRO had what Rijkman Groenink, the current managing board chairman, describes as "the luxury of capi-tal and talent." Back then, he recalls, "the bank faced no real capital constraints and few important resource trade-offs." Thus the board spent very little time, if any, debating strategy or making resource allocation decisions. But when Groenink became chairman in May 2000, ABN AMRO faced significant resource constraints. Global financial markets had consolidated, and stiff competition emerged from the likes of Citigroup, JPMorgan Chase, and ING. Confronted with this new reality, Groenink believed ABN AMRO needed "a new and more-disciplined approach to resource allocation."

An important element of Groenink's approach was to transform the managing board into a decision-making body that truly had clear authority and could be fairly held accountable for the bank's perfor-mance. This transformation required fundamental changes in both the timing and the structure of board meetings. Whereas historically the board met twice a week for three hours to discuss the bank's oper-ations, under the new framework it meets only once a week to discuss operations and then once a month—for a full day—to debate strategy and make important resource allocation decisions. The new meeting calendar reduces the time board members spend together each month (from 24 to 22 hours). But it significantly increases the time dedicated to strategy—from as little as one hour a month to as much as 10.

Since then, ABN AMRO has dramatically improved the effective-ness of its board meetings. The clear delineation between operations time and strategy time allows the board to focus each session and perform both roles better. To improve operating reviews, the bank has installed advanced information and performance-reporting systems that allow the team to monitor results and debate operating issues on an exceptions basis. That has left the board free to adopt many of the other improvements to its strategy sessions that I will describe below.

Focus on decisions, not on discussions

The changes needed to focus a leadership team's meetings more intensely on decision-making can seem almost surprisingly innocuous. At British confectionery and beverage giant Cadbury Schweppes, for example, the chief executive committee approves the company's strategy and investments. The CEC meets for two full days six times a year to debate important strategic and organizational issues. Two small changes have had a big impact on the quality and pace of this group's decision-making capabilities.

First, since 1997, all reading materials have been distributed to participants at least five days before each CEC session. Whenever possible, standard templates are used to display important financial, market, and competitor information. This gives each CEC member time to carefully review materials before the meeting and quickly get up to speed on important issues. Second, a standard cover sheet is included with all materials specifying precisely why people are being asked to read them—for information purposes only, for discussion and debate (in which case, the key issues are highlighted), or for making a decision and deciding a course of action.

Since the purpose of each agenda item is clearly indicated and all materials are reviewed in advance, CEC members can devote meeting time to making decisions on important issues rather than to having those issues explained in lengthy PowerPoint presentations. What's more, the structure imposed by the standard cover sheet has encouraged Cadbury Schweppes executives to deal with many matters outside the meetings—to find other ways to review materials marked "for information purposes" only and to gather input from CEC members before meetings on items marked "for discussion and debate." This reserves even more meeting time for items labeled "action and decision."

Some companies find that shifting the focus of their top management meetings from discussion to decision-making has a wholly transformative effect. That was true at the British bank Barclays, where Matt Barrett spurred a cultural revolution soon after becoming group chief executive in 1999. The bank's executive committee (EXCO), a group of managers representing business and functional silos, had held weekly meetings that amounted to what Barrett calls "bilateral discussions with the CEO with an audience." But Barrett made it clear that he wanted the EXCO to be an integral part of governance and control—to be, in his words, "the linchpin between management and the board of directors." To do that, it had to focus its time on decision-making.

One of the first steps Barrett took was to establish a common ambition for the team—to create "a real passion for performance at Barclays," spurring the EXCO to set the objective of doubling the market value of the bank in five years. Next, EXCO members saw to it that this objective was transmitted to each line of business—to the investment bank, the retail bank, the credit card division, and so on. In this way, it was made clear that each member of the EXCO had a role to play in driving value growth at the bank. Finally, detailed information was developed for each line of business specifying where and how it was creating and destroying value (often at the product and customer level). The establishment of common goals, combined with the generation of such detailed strategic and financial information, allowed Barrett to focus the EXCO on tangible debates about what needed to be done to double the value of the bank. The result has been a marked change in the nature of EXCO meetings. Where once the bank was "drowning in tactical issues," Barrett maintains, "80% of the EXCO's time is now focused on strategic decision-making."

Measure the real value of every item on the agenda

If top managers were presented with five issues, and they knew that resolving one would create 20 times more value than dealing with the other four combined, they would naturally spend their time addressing the issue of highest value. Of course, the importance of agenda items is rarely labeled so explicitly. As a result, top executives

risk wasting valuable time on trivial issues and postponing important decisions, sometimes indefinitely.

Successful companies prioritize the problems and opportunities
on top management's agenda according to the "value at stake"—
that is, according to the impact that resolving each issue will have
on the company's long-term intrinsic value (the net present value
of the company's future cash flows discounted at the appropriate
risk-adjusted cost of capital). This can be done through a broad
sensitivity analysis using the company's valuation model; numeric
precision is not the object of this analysis, only a general understanding. Typically, lower levels of the organization should address
the low value-at-stake issues. Conversely, high value-at-stake issues
should always be on top management's agenda irrespective of organizational boundaries. Identifying items according to their strategic
value makes top management's agenda the critical tool in driving
company performance and translating strategy into action.

Roche, the Swiss drug and diagnostic product maker, is one company that uses this approach particularly effectively. CEO Franz
Humer has created a "decision agenda" comprising the 10 most
important opportunities and problems the company faces. A disciplined process is used to create and update the agenda in which
the value at stake is quantified for each issue. All together, work on
those 10 items takes up more than half of the chief executive committee's time each year. By focusing top managers' time on Roche's
highest-value issues in this way, Humer has transformed the quality
and pace of strategic decision-making at the company.

Get issues off the agenda as quickly as possible

Companies that focus top management on growing long-term value
have just as rigorous a process for getting issues *off* the agenda as
they do for getting the right issues on it in the first place. In other
words, once the right issues are on management's agenda, it's imperative that the team has a clear way to resolve them. Such a process
must include an unambiguous timetable, detailing when and how
team members will reach a decision on each issue and who must be
involved in approving the final strategy.

At Cardinal Health, founder and CEO Bob Walter maintains that "a leader needs to keep people's noses to the grindstone and raise their eyes to the horizon." This view, combined with Walter's natural impatience, has given rise to a leadership model that treats "delay as the worst form of denial." So, all senior managers at the pharmaceutical and medical supply distributor work under a strict decision-making timetable driven from the top. Walter explains: "If you get to the end of a meeting and people ask, 'Did we make a decision on that? Oh, I guess we decided to delay,' then you are in denial. . . . I have a mental clock running at all times that pushes me to move ahead. I try to get everybody else moving ahead as well."

Walter pressures Cardinal's managers to continually ask themselves, "When does this decision need to be made?" and then make sure their timetable will enable them to reach a decision in time. All communications are streamlined—or, as Walter puts it, "crisp"—to focus the team on the most important aspects of a decision. Furthermore, Walter himself keeps a careful check on the decision timetable so that issues get off management's agenda as quickly as possible. This practice facilitates rapid decision-making and prevents overanalysis.

Put real choices on the table

Once the right issues are on the table and the clock is running, the most important requirement for effective strategic decision-making is to present viable options. After all, management can't make choices if it doesn't have real alternatives. In our view, management needs to have at least three alternatives before any strategy should be discussed or approved. These must be real alternatives—not just minor variations on a single theme. But our research suggests that this practice is the exception rather than the rule at most companies. Only 14% of the executives we surveyed were consistently presented with any alternative strategies.

Perhaps no executive has used alternatives more effectively to drive breakout performance than Brian Pitman, former chairman and CEO of the British retail bank Lloyds TSB (and currently on Marakon's board of external advisers). Under his leadership, the bank's market value increased an incredible 40-fold from 1983 to 2001. Pitman would tell his executive team: "There is always a better strategy; we just haven't thought of it yet." Accordingly, he would insist on seeing at least three alternatives from every Lloyds TSB business before approving that business's strategy. "To be confident of what you are accepting," he would say, "you have got to understand what you are rejecting." By forcing a constructive debate about alternatives, Pitman drove a number of fundamental changes in the bank's strategy, impelling the company to exit international markets, establish a low-cost position, and initiate a drive to deliver truly superior customer service. Under his leadership, the search for alternatives was relentless. "The second you believe you have a 'winning strategy,' you are going to be copied," he insists. "You have got to be constantly focused on reinventing your business. . . . It all starts and ends with alternatives."

In considering strategy alternatives, many top management teams find it helpful to separate their discussion of alternatives from their ultimate selection of the best strategy. This practice puts all options on the table before starting the evaluation process. How many times have executives sat through a presentation of a strategic plan or investment proposal knowing that there was another viable course but not knowing whether it had been considered and rejected? That's why companies like ABN AMRO, Cadbury Schweppes, and Boeing often hold a meeting to discuss alternatives before they meet to approve a course of action. Here, "approve" means there are no other appropriate alternatives that the top team hasn't reviewed. And it means that none of the alternatives the team has reviewed is illegal or in conflict with some other strategic initiative at the company.

Separating the generation of strategic alternatives from their evaluation and approval improves the ultimate selection process. When top managers are confident that all alternatives have been thoroughly evaluated, they are much more willing to choose a course of action and allocate the necessary resources—in effect, to make a final decision. There's less chance of rework—the all-too-common scramble at lower levels to generate additional analysis to "satisfy the boss"—and the ultimate choice is more meaningful.

Adopt common decision-making processes and standards

Some top management teams find it difficult to accelerate the pace of decision-making without sacrificing quality, but there are ways to avoid that trade-off. Even if they can't make each decision any faster, they can reach more decisions in the same amount of time by considering more issues in tandem. To do so, companies with superior decision-making capabilities use a common language, methodology, and set of standards for making decisions. This lets them address many issues at once—often outside the team meetings. Individual decisions may not be made any faster in this way, but the team will be able to reach many more decisions each year.

Barclays is a case in point. Barrett believes that much of the improvement in the bank's performance under his leadership has come from increases in both the quality and the quantity of executive committee decisions, which were made possible by a common language and decision-making methodology.

"We have a couple of important standards," Barrett explains. "No self-delusion, and create and sustain competitive advantage or don't do it." All strategic decisions are subject to three tests that are well understood throughout the organization: They must be fact based, alternatives driven, and consequential. By "fact based," Barclays means that opportunities must be identified through a clear understanding of how each Barclays business creates (or could create) shareholder value. Strategic and financial information (the "facts") must be provided to show that there is sufficient value at stake to justify EXCO consideration. By "alternatives driven," Barclays means simply that before any recommendation is made, at least three alternatives must be presented to the EXCO for scrutiny and debate. "Consequential" means that after a decision is reached, it has to be embedded in a business's operating plan, and its subsequent performance must be carefully monitored. Establishing these common standards has effectively expanded the executive committee's capacity to make decisions without sacrificing their quality.

Make decisions stick

Often, the biggest challenge a top management team faces is agreeing on what it agreed to in the meeting. Indeed, unless strategic decisions are translated into something tangible, they can become subject to reinterpretation or, even worse, fall victim to the silent veto.

Like Barclays, several successful companies we studied make the strategic decision-making process consequential by tying resource allocation to strategy approval. At ABN AMRO, Alcan, and Cadbury Schweppes, for example, the outcome of strategic planning is a formal performance contract, which specifies the resources (time, talent, and money) required to execute the strategy, as well as the financial results that management pledges to deliver.

This process makes strategic decisions stick in two ways. First, it forces companies to be clear about what the final decision is. If there is ambiguity about the resources required to execute the strategy or about what results should be expected over time, the leadership team can withhold its approval until those things are nailed down. In effect, tying decisions to resources means the leadership team must formally approve each business unit's strategy. Second, performance contracts make strategy delivery easier to track. A business unit's performance can be monitored relative to the terms of its contract. If the business fails to deliver its contracted level of performance, then the strategy goes back on top management's agenda for reevaluation and eventual course correction. The business units and top management are left with little room for doubt or reinterpretation.

In addition to process solutions like performance contracts, some companies establish norms of behavior for leadership team members to foster greater collaboration and to make decisions stick. When Jim Kilts became CEO of Gillette in 2001, for example, he established just such clear ground rules. One was: "Decisions at Gillette are final. The team is free to debate any decision in staff meetings, but once a decision is reached, there is no more debate—no 'I don't agree with this, but I'll do it anyway' hallway conversations."

To put teeth into the team's norms, Kilts has members rate each other's performance every year—a rating that has a significant impact on their compensation. "Top management compensation used to be based on effort rather than results," Kilts says. "The higher the promise, the better the reward, and the last one in with bad news got off easiest." Now, at the end of each year, the Gillette executive team grades the quality of its decision-making and its overall performance (on a 1-to-5 scale) in this way:

- All team members grade themselves.

- The CEO grades each team member.

- Each team member grades the team overall.

- Each team member grades each of the other team members.

In this way, Kilts and the other members of Gillette's executive team keep the focus on decision-making and encourage individual members to keep their commitments.

If more companies recognized that top management's time was their most precious resource, we would see many more of them adopting the practices I have just described. Strategic planning would not be about off-sites or planning books. It would be a matter of ensuring that the top management team focuses on the most important issues, considers all viable alternatives, and makes the best possible choice in the shortest period of time. Meeting agendas would be systematically managed and continually refreshed so that the right issues came on—and off—the agenda as quickly as possible. In short, strategic planning would be designed to exploit valuable time and drive more and better decisions faster.

Originally published in September 2004. Reprint R0409C

Transient Advantage

by Rita Gunther McGrath

STRATEGY IS STUCK. For too long the business world has been obsessed with the notion of building a sustainable competitive advantage. That idea is at the core of most strategy textbooks; it forms the basis of Warren Buffett's investment strategy; it's central to the success of companies on the "most admired" lists. I'm not arguing that it's a bad idea—obviously, it's marvelous to compete in a way that others can't imitate. And even today there are companies that create a strong position and defend it for extended periods of time—firms such as GE, IKEA, Unilever, Tsingtao Brewery, and Swiss Re. But it's now rare for a company to maintain a truly lasting advantage. Competitors and customers have become too unpredictable, and industries too amorphous. The forces at work here are familiar: the digital revolution, a "flat" world, fewer barriers to entry, globalization.

Strategy *is* still useful in turbulent industries like consumer electronics, fast-moving consumer goods, television, publishing, photography, and . . . well, you get the idea. Leaders in these businesses can compete effectively—but not by sticking to the same old playbook. In a world where a competitive advantage often evaporates in less than a year, companies can't afford to spend months at a time crafting a single long-term strategy. To stay ahead, they need to constantly start new strategic initiatives, building and exploiting many *transient competitive advantages* at once. Though individually temporary, these advantages, as a portfolio, can keep companies in the lead over the long run. Firms that have figured this out—such as

Milliken & Company, a U.S.-based textiles and chemicals company; Cognizant, a global IT services company; and Brambles, a logistics company based in Australia—have abandoned the assumption that stability in business is the norm. They don't even think it should be a goal. Instead, they work to spark continuous change, avoiding dangerous rigidity. They view strategy differently—as more fluid, more customer-centric, less industry-bound. And the ways they formulate it—the lens they use to define the competitive playing field, their methods for evaluating new business opportunities, their approach to innovation—are different as well.

I'm hardly the first person to write about how fast-moving competition changes strategy; indeed, I'm building on the work of Ian MacMillan (a longtime coauthor), Kathleen Eisenhardt, Yves Doz, George Stalk, Mikko Kosonen, Richard D'Aveni, Paul Nunes, and others. However, the thinking in this area—and the reality on the ground—has reached an inflection point. The field of strategy needs to acknowledge what a multitude of practitioners already know: Sustainable competitive advantage is now the exception, not the rule. Transient advantage is the new normal.

The Anatomy of a Transient Advantage

Any competitive advantage—whether it lasts two seasons or two decades—goes through the same life cycle. (See "The wave of transient advantage.") But when advantages are fleeting, firms must rotate through the cycle much more quickly and more often, so they need a deeper understanding of the early and late stages than they would if they were able to maintain one strong position for many years.

A competitive advantage begins with a _launch_ process, in which the organization identifies an opportunity and mobilizes resources to capitalize on it. In this phase a company needs people who are capable of filling in blank sheets of paper with ideas, who are comfortable with experimentation and iteration, and who probably get bored with the kind of structure required to manage a large, complex organization.

In the next phase, _ramp up,_ the business idea is brought to scale. This period calls for people who can assemble the right resources at

Idea in Brief

The dominant idea in the field of strategy—that success consists of establishing a unique competitive position, sustained for long periods of time—is no longer relevant for most businesses. They need to embrace the notion of transient advantage instead, learning to launch new strategic initiatives again and again, and creating a portfolio of advantages that can be built quickly and abandoned just as rapidly. Success will require a new set of operational capabilities.

the right time with the right quality and deliver on the promise of the idea.

Then, if a firm is fortunate, it begins a period of *exploitation,* in which it captures profits and share, and forces competitors to react. At this point a company needs people who are good at M&A, analytical decision-making, and efficiency. Traditional established companies have plenty of talent with this skill set.

Often, the very success of the initiative spawns competition, weakening the advantage. So the firm has to *reconfigure* what it's doing to keep the advantage fresh. For reconfigurations, a firm needs people who aren't afraid to radically rethink business models or resources.

In some cases the advantage is completely eroded, compelling the company to begin a *disengagement* process in which resources are extracted and reallocated to the next-generation advantage. To manage this process, you need people who can be candid and tough-minded and can make emotionally difficult decisions.

For sensible reasons, companies with any degree of maturity tend to be oriented toward the exploitation phase of the life cycle. But as I've suggested, they need different skills, metrics, and people to manage the tasks inherent in each stage of an advantage's development. And if they're creating a pipeline of competitive advantages, the challenge is even more complex, because they'll need to orchestrate many activities that are inconsistent with one another.

Milliken & Company is a fascinating example of an organization that managed to overcome the competitive forces that annihilated its industry (albeit over a longer time period than some companies today will be granted). By 1991 virtually all of Milliken's traditional competitors had vanished, victims of a surge in global competition

The wave of transient advantage

Companies in high-velocity industries must learn to cycle rapidly through the stages of competitive advantage. They also need the capacity to develop and manage a pipeline of initiatives, since many will be short-lived.

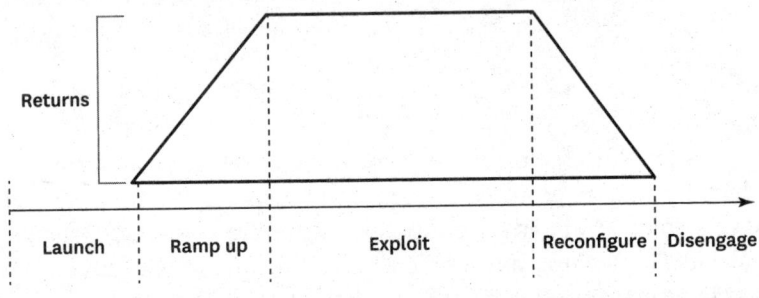

that moved the entire business of textile manufacturing to Asia. In Milliken, one sees very clearly the pattern of entering new, more promising arenas while disengaging from older, exhausted ones. Ultimately, the company exited most of its textile lines, but it did not do so suddenly. It gradually shut down American plants, starting in the 1980s and continuing through 2009. (Every effort was made, as best I can tell, to reallocate workers who might have suffered as a result.) At the same time the company was investing in international expansion, new technologies, and new markets, including forays into new arenas to which its capabilities provided access. As a result, a company that had been largely focused on textiles and chemicals through the 1960s, and advanced materials and flameproof products through the 1990s, had become a leader in specialty materials and high-IP specialty chemicals by the 2000s.

Facing the Brutal Truth

In a world that values exploitation, people on the front lines are rarely rewarded for telling powerful senior executives that a competitive advantage is fading away. Better to shore up an existing advantage for as long as possible, until the pain becomes so obvious that there is no choice. That's what happened at IBM, Sony, Nokia, Kodak, and a host of other firms that got themselves into terrible trouble, despite ample early warnings from those working with customers.

To compete in a transient-advantage economy, you must be willing to honestly assess whether current advantages are at risk. Ask yourself which of these statements is true of your company:

- I don't buy my own company's products or services.

- We're investing at the same or higher levels and not getting better margins or growth in return.

- Customers are finding cheaper or simpler solutions to be "good enough."

- Competition is emerging from places we didn't expect.

- Customers are no longer excited about what we have to offer.

- We're not considered a top place to work by the people we'd like to hire.

- Some of our very best people are leaving.

- Our stock is perpetually undervalued.

If you nodded in agreement with four or more of these, that's a clear warning that you may be facing imminent erosion.

But it isn't enough to recognize a problem. You also have to abandon many of the traditional notions about competitive strategy that will exacerbate the challenge of strategy reinvention.

Seven Dangerous Misconceptions

Most executives working in a high-velocity setting know perfectly well that they need to change their mode of operation. Often, though, deeply embedded assumptions can lead companies into traps. Here are the ones I see most often.

The first-mover trap

This is the belief that being first to market and owning assets create a sustainable position. In some businesses—like aircraft engines or mining—that's still true. But in most industries a first-mover advantage doesn't last.

The superiority trap

Almost any early-stage technology, process, or product won't be as effective as something that's been honed and polished for years. Because of that disparity, many companies don't see the need to invest in improving their established offerings—until the upstart innovations mature, by which time it's often too late for the incumbents.

The quality trap

Many businesses in exploit mode stick with a level of quality higher than customers are prepared to pay for. When a cheaper, simpler offer is good enough, customers will abandon the incumbent.

The hostage-resources trap

In most companies, executives running big, profitable businesses get to call the shots. These people have no incentive to shift resources to new ventures. I remember holding a Nokia product that was remarkably similar to today's iPad—in about 2004. It hooked up to the internet, accessed web pages, and even had a rudimentary app constellation. Why did Nokia never capitalize on this groundbreaking innovation? Because the company's emphasis was on mass-market phones, and resource allocation decisions were made accordingly.

The white-space trap

When I ask executives about the biggest barriers to innovation, I often hear, "Well, these things fall between the cracks of our organizational structure." When opportunities don't fit their structure, firms often simply forgo them instead of making the effort to reorganize. For instance, a product manufacturer might pass up potentially profitable moves into services because they require coordination of activities along a customer's experience rather than by product line.

The empire-building trap

In a lot of companies, the more assets and employees you manage, the better. This system promotes hoarding, bureaucracy building, and fierce defense of the status quo; it inhibits experimentation, iterative learning, and risk-taking. And it causes employees who like to do new things to leave.

The sporadic-innovation trap

Many companies do not have a system for creating a pipeline of new advantages. As a result, innovation is an on-again, off-again process that is driven by individuals, making it extraordinarily vulnerable to swings in the business cycle.

The assessment "Is Your Company Prepared for the Transient-Advantage Economy?" at the end of this chapter will give you a sense of whether your organization is vulnerable to these traps.

Strategy for Transient Advantage: The New Playbook

Companies that want to create a portfolio of transient advantages need to make eight major shifts in the way that they operate.

1. Think about arenas, not industries

One of the more cherished ideas in traditional management is that by looking at data about other firms like yours, you can uncover the right strategy for your organization. Indeed, one of the most influential strategy frameworks, Michael Porter's five forces model, assumes that you are mainly comparing your company to others in a similar industry. In today's environment, where industry lines are quickly blurring, this can blindside you.

I've seen untraditional competitors take companies by surprise over and over again. In the 1980s, for instance, no money-center bank even saw the threat posed by Merrill Lynch's new cash-management accounts, because they weren't offered by any bank.

ts flew out the door before the banks realized what
in recent years, the phenomenon has become
common. Google's moves into phone operating systems and
online video have created consternation in traditional phone businesses; retailers like Walmart have begun edging into health care;
and the entire activity of making payments is being disrupted by
players from a variety of industries, including mobile phone operators, internet credit providers, and swipe-card makers.

Today strategy involves orchestrating competitive moves in what
I call "arenas." An arena is a combination of a customer segment, an
offer, and a place in which that offer is delivered. It isn't that industries aren't relevant anymore; it's just that industry-level analysis
doesn't give you the full picture. Indeed, the very notion of a transient competitive advantage is less about making more money than
your industry peers, as conventional definitions would have it, and
more about responding to customers' "jobs to be done" (as Tony
Ulwick would call it) in a given space.

2. Set broad themes, and then let people experiment

The shift to a focus on arenas means that you can't analyze your way
to an advantage with armies of junior staffers or consultants anymore.
Today's gifted strategists examine the data, certainly, but they also
use advanced pattern recognition, direct observation, and the inter-
pretation of weak signals in the environment to set broad themes.
Within those themes, they free people to try different approaches
and business models. Cognizant, for instance, clearly spells out the
competitive terrain it would like to claim but permits people on the
ground considerable latitude within that framework. "The Future of
Work" is Cognizant's umbrella term for a host of services intended to
help clients rethink their business models, reinvent their workforces,
and rewire their operations—all with the firm's assistance, of course.

3. Adopt metrics that support entrepreneurial growth

When advantages come and go, conventional metrics can effectively kill off innovations by imposing decision rules that make no
sense. The net present value rule, for instance, assumes that you will

complete every project you start, that advantages will last for quite a while, and that there will even be a "terminal value" left once they are gone. It leads companies to underinvest in new opportunities.

Instead, firms can use the logic of "real options" to evaluate new moves. A real option is a small investment that conveys the right, but not the obligation, to make a more significant commitment in the future. It allows the organization to learn through trial and error. Consider the way Intuit has made experimentation a core strategic process, amplifying by orders of magnitude its ability to venture into new spaces and try new things. As Kaaren Hanson, the company's vice president of design innovation, said at a recent conference at Columbia Business School, the important thing is to "fall in love with the problem you are trying to solve" rather than with the solution, and to be comfortable with iteration as you work toward the answer.

4. Focus on experiences and solutions to problems

As barriers to entry tumble, product features can be copied in an instant. Even service offerings in many industries have become commoditized. Once a company has demonstrated that demand for something exists, competitors quickly move in. What customers crave—and few companies provide—are well-designed experiences and complete solutions to their problems. Unfortunately, many companies are so internally focused that they're oblivious to the customer's experience. You call up your friendly local cable company or telephone provider and get connected to a robot. The robot wants to know your customer number, which you dutifully provide. Eventually, the robot decides that your particular problem is too difficult and hands you over to a live person. What's the first thing the person wants to know? Yup, your customer number. It's symptomatic of the disjointed and fragmented way most complex organizations handle customers.

Companies skilled at exploiting transient advantage put themselves in their customers' place and consider the outcome customers are trying to achieve. Australia's Brambles has done a really great job of this even though it is in a seemingly dull industry (managing the logistics of pallets and other containers). The company realized that one of grocers' biggest costs was the labor required to shelve goods delivered to their stores. Brambles designed a solution: plastic bins that can be filled by growers right in the fields and lifted directly from pallets and placed on shelves, from which customers can help themselves. It has cut labor costs significantly. Better yet, fruits and vegetables arrive at the point of purchase in better shape because they aren't manhandled repeatedly as they go from field to box to truck to warehouse to storage room to shelf. Although seemingly low-tech, this initiative and others like it have generated substantial profits and steady growth for the company—not to mention customers' appreciation.

5. Build strong relationships and networks
One of the few barriers to entry that remains powerful in a transient-advantage context has to do with people and their personal networks. Indeed, evidence suggests that the most successful and sought-after employees are those with the most robust networks. Realizing that strong relationships with customers are a profound source of advantage, many companies have begun to invest in communities and networks as a way of deepening ties with customers. Intuit, for example, has created a space on its website where customers can interact, solve one another's problems, and share ideas. The company goes so far as to recognize exemplary problem solvers with special titles and short profiles of them on the site. Amazon and TripAdvisor both make contributions from their communities a core part of the value they offer customers. And of course, social networks have the power to enhance or destroy a firm's credibility in nanoseconds as customers enjoy an unprecedented ability to connect with one another.

Firms that are skilled at managing networks are also notable for the way they preserve important relationships. Infosys, for instance, is choosy about which customers it will serve, but it maintains a 97% customer retention rate. Sagentia, a technical consultancy in the UK, is extremely conscientious about making sure that people who are let go remain on good terms with the firm and land well in new positions. Even at a large industrial company like GE, the senior leaders spend inordinate amounts of time building and preserving relationships with other firms.

6. Avoid brutal restructuring; learn healthy disengagement

In researching firms that effectively navigate the transient-advantage economy, I was struck by how seldom they engaged in restructuring, downsizing, or mass firings. Instead, many of them seemed to continually adjust and readjust their resources. At Infosys, I was told, people don't really believe in "chopping things off." Rather, when an initiative is wound down, they say it "finds its way to insignificance."

Sometimes, of course, downsizing or sudden shifts can't be avoided. The challenge then is disengaging from a business in the least destructive, most beneficial way. Netflix's efforts to get out of the DVD-shipping business and into streaming movies, which its management passionately believes represents the future, offer an interesting lesson in the wrong way to do this. In 2011 the company's management made two decisions that infuriated customers. It imposed a massive price increase across the board, and it split the DVD and streaming businesses into two separate organizations, which forced customers to duplicate their efforts to find and purchase movies. Let's assume that Netflix's leaders are right that eventually the DVD part of the business will shrivel up. How might the firm have exited more gracefully?

Preparing customers to transition away from old advantages is a lot like getting them to adopt a new product, but in reverse. Not all customers will be prepared to move at the same rate. There is a sequence to which customers you should transition first, second, and so on.

If, rather than raising prices for everybody, Netflix had selectively offered price discounts to those who would drop the DVD service, it would have moved that segment over to the new model. Then it could have gone to the "light user" DVD consumers and suggested that instead of getting a new DVD anytime they wanted it, they would get one once a month, say, for the same price. If they wanted the instant service, their prices would go up. That would shift another group to lower DVD usage. Then when those segments started to realize that all-streaming wasn't so bad, Netflix could have instituted the big price increase for the mainstream buyer. The point is that in trying to force many customers to move faster than they were prepared to, the company enraged them.

7. Get systematic about early-stage innovation

If advantages eventually disappear, it only makes sense to have a process for filling your pipeline with new ones. This in turn means that, rather than being an on-again, off-again mishmash of projects, your innovation process needs to be carefully orchestrated.

Companies that innovate proficiently manage the process in similar ways. They have a governance structure suitable for innovation: They set aside a separate budget and staff for innovation and allow senior leaders to make go or no-go decisions about it outside the planning processes for individual businesses. The earmarked innovation budget, which gets allocated across projects, means that new initiatives don't have to compete with established businesses for resources. Such companies also have a strong sense of how innovations fit into the larger portfolio, and a line of sight to initiatives in all different stages. They hunt systematically for opportunities, usually searching beyond the boundaries of the firm and its R&D department and figuring out what customers are trying to accomplish and how the firm can help them do it.

8. Experiment, iterate, learn

As I've said for many years, a big mistake companies make all the time is planning new ventures with the same approaches they use for more-established businesses. Instead, they need to focus on experimentation and learning, and be prepared to make a shift or change emphasis as new discoveries happen. The discovery phase is followed by business model definition and incubation, in which a project takes the shape of an actual business and may begin pilot tests or serving customers. Only once the initiative is relatively stable and healthy is it ramped up. All too often, in their haste to get commercial traction, companies rush through this phase; as a result, whatever product they introduce has critical flaws. They also spend way too much money before testing the critical assumptions that will spell success or failure.

Leadership as Orchestration

No leader could cognitively handle the complexity of scores of individual arenas, all at slightly different stages of development. What great leaders do is figure out some key directional guidelines, put in place good processes for core activities such as innovation, and use their influence over a few crucial inflection points to direct the flow of activities in the organization. This requires a new kind of leader— one who initiates conversations that question, rather than reinforce, the status quo. A strong leader seeks contrasting opinions and honest disagreement. Diversity increasingly becomes a tool for picking up signals that things may be changing. Broader constituencies may well become involved in the strategy process.

Finally, transient-advantage leaders recognize the need for speed. Fast and roughly right decision-making will replace deliberations that are precise but slow. In a world where advantages last for five minutes, you can blink and miss the window of opportunity.

One thing about strategy hasn't changed: It still requires making tough choices about what to do and, even more important, what not to do. Even though you are orchestrating scores of arenas, you can do only so many things. So defining where you want to compete, how you intend to win, and how you are going to move from advantage to advantage is critical. While we might be tempted to throw up our hands and say that strategy is no longer useful, I think the opposite conclusion is called for. It's more important than ever. It just isn't about the status quo any longer.

Originally published in June 2013. Reprint R1306C

Is Your Company Prepared for the Transient-Advantage Economy?

TO SEIZE TRANSIENT ADVANTAGES, companies need a new mode of operation. The diagnostic below can help pinpoint areas where change is required. Simply position your organization's current way of working between the two statements in the assessment. If you score in the lower part of the range in an area, you might want to take a hard look at it.

Focused on extending existing advantages								Capable of coping with transient advantage
Budgets, people, and other resources are largely controlled by heads of established businesses.	1	2	3	4	5	6	7	Critical resources are controlled by a separate group that doesn't run businesses.
We tend to extend our established advantages if we can.	1	2	3	4	5	6	7	We tend to move out of an established advantage early, with the goal of moving on to something new.
We don't have a process for disengaging from a business.	1	2	3	4	5	6	7	We have a systematic way of exiting businesses.
Disengagements tend to be painful and difficult.	1	2	3	4	5	6	7	Disengagements are just part of the normal business cycle.
We try to avoid failures, even in uncertain situations.	1	2	3	4	5	6	7	We recognize that failures are unavoidable and try to learn from them.
We budget annually or for even longer.	1	2	3	4	5	6	7	We budget in quick cycles, either quarterly or on a rolling basis.
We like to stick to plans once they are formulated.	1	2	3	4	5	6	7	We are comfortable changing our plans as new information comes in.

	Left statement	1	2	3	4	5	6	7	Right statement
✳	We emphasize optimization in our approach to asset utilization.	1	2	3	4	5	6	7	We emphasize flexibility in our approach to asset utilization.
	Innovation is an on-again, off-again process.	1	2	3	4	5	6	7	Innovation is an ongoing, systematic core process for us.
	It's difficult for us to pull resources from a successful business to fund more uncertain opportunities.	1	2	3	4	5	6	7	It's quite normal for us to pull resources from a successful business to fund more uncertain opportunities.
✗	Our best people spend most of their time solving problems and handling crises.	1	2	3	4	5	6	7	Our best people spend most of their time working on new opportunities for our organization.
	We try to keep our organizational structure relatively stable and to fit new ideas into the existing structure.	1	2	3	4	5	6	7	We reorganize when new opportunities require a different structure.
	We tend to emphasize analysis over experimentation.	1	2	3	4	5	6	7	We tend to emphasize experimentation over analysis.
	It isn't easy to be candid with our senior leaders when something goes wrong.	1	2	3	4	5	6	7	We find it very easy to be candid with senior leaders when something goes wrong.

Breaking Down the Barriers to Innovation

by Scott D. Anthony, Paul Cobban, Rahul Nair, and Natalie Painchaud

TO CATALYZE INNOVATION, companies have invested billions in internal venture capital, incubators, accelerators, and field trips to Silicon Valley. Yet according to a McKinsey survey, 94% of executives are dissatisfied with their firms' innovation performance. Across industries, one survey after another has found the same thing: Businesses just aren't getting the impact they want, despite all their spending. Why? We believe that it's because they've failed to address a huge underlying obstacle: the day-to-day routines and rituals that stifle innovation.

Fortunately, it's possible to "hack" this problem. Drawing on the behavioral-change literature and on our experiences working with dozens of global companies, including DBS, Southeast Asia's biggest bank, we've devised a practical way to break bad habits that squelch innovation and to develop new ones that inspire it.

Like most hacks, our approach isn't expensive, though it does take time and energy. It involves setting up interventions we call BEANs, shorthand for *behavior enablers, artifacts,* and *nudges.* Behavior enablers are tools or processes that make it easier for people to do something different. Artifacts—things you can see and touch—support the new behavior. And nudges, a tactic drawn from behavioral science, promote change through indirect suggestion and reinforcement. Though the acronym may sound a bit glib, we've found that it's simple and memorable in a way that's useful for organizations trying to develop better habits.

In this article we'll describe a variety of BEANs that firms have used to unleash innovation, the characteristics that make them effective, and how your organization can develop and implement its own BEANs. But first we'll briefly examine the behaviors that drive innovation and the barriers that thwart it.

Innovation Behaviors and Blockers

To us, innovation doesn't mean mere inventiveness. In our work we define it as "something different that creates value." It isn't just the purview of engineers and scientists, nor is it limited to new-product development. Processes can be innovated. Marketing approaches can too. Something different can be a big breakthrough, but it can also be an everyday improvement that makes the complicated a bit simpler or the expensive more affordable.

In our work and research, we've found that the most innovative organizations exhibit five key behaviors: They always assume there's a better way to do things. They focus on deeply understanding customers' stated and unstated needs and desires. They collaborate across and beyond the organization, actively cross-pollinating. They recognize that success requires experimentation, rapid iteration, and frequent failure. Last, they empower people to take considered risks, voice dissenting opinions, and seek needed resources.

None of those behaviors is surprising. It's just puzzling that they aren't more common. After all, as children, most of us were creative, curious, collaborative, and risk-taking. But once we went to school and, later, to work, those behaviors got quashed. Students and employees are taught there's a right way to do things. That raising questions and expressing dissent, even benignly, is risky. As people learn those rules, the innovation muscles that were toned in their youth atrophy. That may explain why kindergarten graduates generally outperform new MBAs on "the marshmallow challenge,"

Idea in Brief

The Challenge

Companies' investments in innovation are stymied by the day-to-day routines and habits that stifle original thinking.

The Solution

Leadership needs to identify these innovation blockers and neutralize them with interventions called "BEANs"—behavior enablers, artifacts, and nudges.

The Outcome

The bank DBS used this approach to unleash innovation at a tech-development center. Engagement scores rose 20%, and the center was named a great place to innovate.

a timed competition to use spaghetti, tape, and string to build the tallest structure that will support a marshmallow on top.

Ask executives what stands in the way of innovation, and they'll point to real barriers, such as a lack of time (few executives or organizations have slack capacity to spend on new thinking); the perception that doing things differently produces no benefits, just costs (and possibly punishment); a lack of innovation skills; and a lack of infrastructure for bringing ideas to fruition. But one of the biggest impediments is organizational inertia. As an executive once said to us, businesses are "organized to deliver predictable, reliable results—and that's exactly the problem." A major paradox managers face is that the systems that enable success with today's model reinforce behaviors that are inconsistent with discovering tomorrow's model.

If you don't address inertia, efforts to eliminate other blockers won't work. Give people more time in an environment stifled by inertia, and they'll simply have more time to do things the old way; give them new skills, and those will go to waste if they don't fit with existing routines. Fortunately, you can combat both inertia and other blockers with BEANs. Now let's look at an initiative that did just that.

Breaking Down Innovation Barriers at DBS

When Piyush Gupta took over as CEO of DBS, in 2009, he began a multipronged effort to transform it from a stodgy, regulated bank into an agile technology company—or, as he put it, "a 27,000-person

startup." Once mocked locally as "Damn Bloody Slow" (for its noto-
riously long lines), DBS is now considered a global digital leader in
financial services, and in 2019 it became the first bank to simultaneously hold the titles "Bank of the Year" (*The Banker*), "Best Bank in
the World" (*Global Finance*), and "World's Best Bank" (*Euromoney*).

But back in 2016, DBS was still on its journey. When its top leaders
gathered in Singapore to talk about how the bank was progressing,
all agreed that though it had made headway, much work remained.
In their discussion they identified dysfunctional meetings as a
major blocker that entrenched organizational inertia and hindered
innovation. Most meetings at DBS could charitably be described as
inefficient. They would often start and run late, eating up time that
leaders could otherwise have spent on innovation. Sometimes decisions were made, and sometimes they were not. People would dutifully arrive at meetings without a clear sense of why they were there.
Some participants were active, but many sat in defensive silence. It's
this last point that's most salient. Meetings, leadership concluded,
were suppressing diverse voices and reinforcing the status quo.

To change that, DBS introduced a BEAN it called MOJO. It was
informed by research at Google that showed that equal share of voice
and psychological safety were critical to high-performing, highly
innovative project teams. MOJO promotes efficient, effective, open,
and collaborative meetings. The MO is the meeting owner, who's
responsible for ensuring that the meeting has a clear agenda, that
it starts and ends on time, and that all attendees are given an equal
say. The JO—or joyful observer—is assigned to help the meeting run
crisply and to encourage broad participation. The JO, for example,
has the authority to call a "phone jenga" that requires all attendees
to put their phones in a pile on the table. Perhaps most important, at
the meeting's end, the JO holds the MO accountable, providing frank
feedback about how things went and how the MO can improve. Even
when the JO is junior, he or she is explicitly authorized to be direct
with the MO. The presence of an observer and the knowledge that
feedback is coming nudge the MO to be mindful of meeting behavior.

This approach, supported by physical reminders in meeting rooms
(small cards, wall art, and fun paper cubes that can be tossed around)

and a range of measurement and tracking tools, has had a power-ful impact. Meetings at DBS no longer run late, saving an estimated 500,000 employee hours to date. Meeting effectiveness, as gauged by ongoing employee surveys, has doubled, and the percentage of employees who say they have an equal share of voice in meetings has jumped from 40% to 90%. Improved efficiency and effectiveness doesn't mean meetings have become dull, however. Living up to their moniker (which reinforces a broader effort at DBS to "make banking joyful"), JOs have even been known to give their feedback in verse. And legends have spread. At one meeting the observer bravely told a senior executive who had lost his cool that the blowup had shut down all discussion. The executive welcomed the feedback, promis-ing to do better next time. It's a story that still circulates, reinforcing the behavioral change DBS hoped to drive with MOJO.

The Keys to Effective BEANs

Over the decades a lot of research has examined why it's so hard for people to break bad habits. Recently, popular books exploring the problem—such as *Switch,* by Chip and Dan Heath; *Nudge,* by Richard Thaler and Cass Sunstein; *The Power of Habit,* by Charles Duhigg; and *Thinking, Fast and Slow,* by Daniel Kahneman—have offered readers a range of practical tools to help. In developing the BEANs solution, we've built on the insights of those academics and prac-titioners, who've consistently found that it's critical to engage both people's rational, logical side and their emotional, intuitive side. We also drew ideas from long-standing programs like Alcoholics Anon-ymous and Weight Watchers, which use a combination of mantras, nudges, and social interactions to change people's patterns, and from the science of motivation, which describes how goal setting, achievement, and social comparison and encouragement reinforce desired behaviors.

In our own research we collected some 130 examples of interven-tions that promoted better innovation habits, which we found either at clients we were working with or by reading through case stud-ies from the Innovation Leader information service and corporate cultural documents compiled by Tettra, a Boston-area startup. Then we and a team from Innosight analyzed those interventions and tested them at a variety of organizations. We determined that successful BEANs typically are:

Simple
Interventions that are easy to adopt and remember gain traction much more quickly.

Fun
When an activity is engaging and social, it's intrinsically rewarding, which makes people more likely to do it—something the science of motivation has long recognized.

Trackable
The ability to monitor performance and compare it against that of others is a powerful motivator. (This is why activity trackers like Fitbit have helped many develop better exercise habits.) So it's critical for BEANs to include a mechanism for measuring their results.

Practical
The best BEANs are smoothly integrated into existing meetings and processes and don't require major changes or entirely new routines.

Reinforced
People often need physical and digital reminders to keep using the new habits.

Organizationally consistent
One of the most cited papers in the change literature is Steven Kerr's 1995 classic "On the Folly of Rewarding A, While Hoping for B." Effective BEANs don't encourage people to do one thing if the company punishes them for that behavior or rewards them for something else.

You can see how all these characteristics come together in MOJO. Another example of a well-crafted BEAN from DBS is the Gandalf scholarship. While Gandalf is the wizard in J.R.R. Tolkien's Lord of the Rings series, the scholarship's name also references DBS's aspiration to be compared to the digital technology giants Google, Apple, Netflix, Amazon, LinkedIn, and Facebook; plop DBS between Netflix and Amazon and you get the acronym. Any employee can apply to receive S$1,000 (about US$740) to spend on a project of his or her choice—a course, books, a conference—that supports DBS's goal of becoming a learning organization that constantly questions the status quo. The only condition is that winners must teach what they've discovered to their colleagues. As of the fall of 2019, the bank had granted more than 100 scholarships in areas from artificial intelligence to storytelling for managers, with the average recipient teaching close to an additional 300 people. DBS has recorded many of these "teach-backs" and posted them on an online channel with related articles and other information, creating virtual artifacts that have been viewed more than 10,000 times. The bank estimates that each dollar it spends on the scholarships has a positive impact on 30 times as many employees as a dollar spent on traditional training does.

Another good example of a BEAN comes from the Tata Group, India's largest conglomerate. Every year the company holds a celebration honoring innovation accomplishments across its sprawling collection of business units, which range from tea to IT consulting to automobiles. One of the most coveted awards given at that gathering is called Dare to Try. As the name connotes, it goes to a team that failed but in an intelligent way. In the company's words, "Showcasing a growing culture of risk-taking and perseverance across Tata companies . . . [Dare to Try] recognizes and rewards novel, daring and seriously attempted ideas that did not achieve the desired results." Dare to Try is a substantial program, attracting hundreds of applications annually. Promotions for it help nudge innovative behaviors like embracing risk and tolerating failure. The award itself—a trophy—and the high-visibility public summary of the event are artifacts that effectively reinforce Tata's innovation culture.

Getting Granular About Innovation Behaviors

TOO FREQUENTLY, EXECUTIVES SAY THEY WANT TO BOOST INNOVATION but aren't specific about what that means. Organizations need to get precise about the behaviors they'd like to see. A good approach is to have employees in focus groups on innovation supply endings to the question "Wouldn't it be great if we . . ." Below are examples of various kinds of suggestions that have been generated in such brainstorming sessions:

Questioning the Status Quo

- Were perpetually paranoid about the future?
- Kept an open mind, constantly asking "What if?"
- Avoided shutting down new ideas by saying "This is the way we do things here"?
- Adopted a problem-solver, versus a fault-finder, mindset?

Focusing Intensely on Customers

- Spent more time with customers to understand their jobs to be done?
- Regularly created customer profiles and customer journeys?
- Ensured all solutions were rooted in addressing key customer needs and problems?
- Had deep insight into how customers made decisions between different solutions?

Collaborating Better

- Built cross-functional teams with expertise and viewpoints from different parts of the organization?

How to Build a BEAN

While many BEANs, such as MOJO, have sprung up organically, we've created a three-step process companies can use to develop them. We've tested and refined this process through repeated application at DBS and other organizations in a range of industries.

- Emphasized collective, versus individual, goals?
- Were transparent and frank while remaining respectful?
- Provided visibility and transparency on initiatives?

Experimenting

- Planned for different scenarios and alternative outcomes?
- Constantly asked ourselves, "What don't we know?" and "How can we learn more?"
- Designed experiments to learn more about key assumptions?
- Rewarded teams for intelligent failure?

Empowering

- Trusted more junior employees to carry out tasks without having to get approval?
- Looked for ways people can bring ideas forward or speak up when something isn't working?
- Owned the outcomes of our decisions without shirking responsibility or playing the blame game?
- Set teams up for success by removing obstacles and providing resources and support?

Several of the tests took place at a technology development center in Hyderabad, India, that DBS had set up as part of its digital transformation. The new center was taking over previously outsourced operations such as the design and support of customer-facing mobile applications, and it presented the company with the opportunity to build a more entrepreneurial culture from scratch.

The center's office design mimicked what you'd see at any hot young tech venture, with open space, foosball tables, snack bars, and the like. Its recruitment processes, borrowed from innovative companies like Netflix, were designed to attract distinctive talent. But when the lights went on, it quickly became clear that employees' day-to-day experiences there had little of that startup feeling. The engineers fell into well-worn routines, working methodically and avoiding fast-paced experimentation. While employee engagement scores weren't terrible, they were notably short of DBS's aspiration.

To turn things around, a group of Innosight consultants and DBS Technology & Operations change agents (which we'll call the culture team) decided to develop BEANs that would disrupt the unwanted habits and promote new and better ones.

Step 1. Specify the desired characteristics

First the team outlined what kind of organizational traits it wanted, describing a culture that would be agile, learning-oriented, customer-obsessed, data-driven, and experimental. It then listed behaviors under each of them. For example, under "experimental" were aspirational statements such as "We rapidly test new ideas," "We believe in lean experimentation," and "We fail cheap, we fail fast, and we learn even faster."

Step 2. Identify blockers

Next the team looked for things that were getting in the way of the innovative behaviors. To uncover these, members sat in on staff meetings, conducted diagnostic surveys, interviewed center employees one-on-one in confidence, and reviewed "day in the life" journals that developers kept for a week.

Among other issues, the team found that many employees felt they lacked context for their work—an understanding of how their project fit with the broader strategy and what was expected of each person working on the project and of the project overall. Some employees also felt that surfacing problems was taboo, and so they stewed in silent frustration. And some simply felt stretched so thin in their day-to-day work that they lacked time to experiment.

Context + time

Note that the team was very precise in describing the behaviors it was seeking and their blockers. This is critical; if you don't do this when developing BEANs, you may end up with ersatz blockers or laundry lists that are difficult to tackle. A simple way to identify specific changes you'd like to see is to gather groups of employees and ask them to complete two sentences: "Wouldn't it be great if we . . ." (which surfaces the behaviors; see the sidebar "Getting Granular About Innovation Behaviors") and "But we don't because . . ." (which helps pinpoint the blockers).

Step 3. Come up with interventions

Last the culture team designed ways to eliminate the blockers. To get things going, it facilitated a pair of two-day workshops with senior leaders, one in Hyderabad and the other in Singapore. After discussing the desired behaviors and their blockers, participants broke into small groups for structured brainstorming. Each group was given examples of BEANs from other organizations for inspiration (see the sidebar "BEANs Across Businesses") and, to devise new ones, used a simple template that had the group specify the behaviors sought, the habits blocking them, and the enablers and nudges that would help employees break through them. All the participants then reassembled to review 15 proposed BEANs and vote on a few to implement.

Here are three interventions that were created to tackle lack of context, voice, and time at the center:

Lack of context

This blocker reinforced employees' sense that their business-as-usual approach was good enough. The BEAN targeting it was a "culture canvas" inspired by Alexander Osterwalder and Yves Pigneur's canvas that maps out the key elements of a business model. The culture canvas is likewise a simple one-page, poster-size template. On it, project teams articulate their business goals and codify team roles and norms. Filling it out helps them gain a clearer sense of expectations, organizational context, and who does what. Giving teams clarity about their goals and the scope to push boundaries further empowers their entrepreneurial spirit. The resulting physical

BEANs Across Businesses

WE'VE IDENTIFIED MORE THAN 100 EXAMPLES of behavior enablers, artifacts, and nudges at work within organizations across industries. While they're all very different, they all serve the purpose of breaking undesirable organizational habits and encouraging new ones. Here are some of our favorites.

Offer a Kickbox

Organization: Adobe

Goal: Encourage experimentation and simplify innovation

Description: Employees apply to receive a red "kickbox" that contains do-it-yourself innovation training, including exercises to perform and a checklist for developing a new product or service idea and pitching it to management. It also contains a prepaid $1,000 debit card to use in validating the concept.

Create a Fail Wall

Organization: Spotify

Goal: Eliminate fear of failure and learn from mistakes

Description: The "fail wall"—a whiteboard with Post-its that publicly celebrates project failures—serves as the starting point for engineering-team postmortems that examine what has been learned and how to prevent similar failures in the future.

Conduct a Premortem

Organization: Atlassian

Goal: Identify threats to new initiatives and develop a defense against them

Description: Before starting a project, teams meet to discuss how it could fail, doing a seven-step exercise that includes a structured cross-examination

---

artifact, which includes photos and signatures of members, serves as a visual reminder of teams' commitments.

Lack of voice

A BEAN called "team temp" was devised to liberate employees to speak up when they saw problems. The web-based app, to be used (in which a group arguing the "success" case questions a group arguing the "failure" case and vice versa), voting to gauge risk severity, assigning risk "owners," and planning how to minimize threats.

Play Lunch Roulette

Organization: Boehringer Ingelheim

Goal: Encourage collaboration and cross-pollination

Description: Lunch roulette is a company website that randomly pairs employees for meals. Participants select a date and a location, click a "match me" button, and simply show up with open minds and a willingness to network.

Go Live from Day One

Organization: Airbnb

Goal: Empower employees with a sense of purpose and responsibility

Description: During the first day of Airbnb's orientation boot camp, engineers are encouraged to push code directly to the website.

Use Games to Develop Leaders

Organization: Tasty Catering

Goal: Help employees think and act like owners

Description: Associates, all of whom are given full visibility into the organization's financials, play a weekly game in which each makes a forecast for a line in the P&L. The projections are then compared with the actual figures. Winners are celebrated and deviations are analyzed, feeding into efforts to identify patterns and generate ideas for further boosting performance.

---

at the first meeting of the week, gauges a project team's mood by inviting members to anonymously enter a score from 1 (highly negative) to 10 (highly positive) and pick a word to describe how they're feeling. This quickly reveals if the team has an issue (a string of 1s and 2s is pretty telling) and prompts a discussion—led by the team leader—about what's going on and how it can be addressed. Because the app tracks team sentiment over time, it also gauges whether interventions are working.

Lack of time

To bust this blocker, the culture team created the "70:20:10" BEAN. Inspired by Google's practices, it gives software developers explicit permission to spend 70% of their time on day-to-day work, 20% on work-improvement ideas, and 10% on experiments and pet projects. By formally freeing up chunks of time for unspecified experimentation, 70:20:10 encourages innovative thinking. To reinforce it, the culture team also created a ritual in which developers shared the learnings of their experimental projects with one another.

These and the other BEANs selected were initially tested by pilot teams in Hyderabad. Their impact was carefully measured, improvements were made, ineffective BEANs were discarded, and effective ones were rolled out more broadly and tracked. As a result of the 70:20:10 BEAN, for example, teams automated several manual processes, shaving man-hours off key tasks, and developed other innovations. (The initial version of an app to track and improve MOJO results came out of one developer's time for experimentation.) Meanwhile, leaders increased the amount of time they spent walking the halls and modeling the new ways of working.

A year after the interventions began, employee surveys showed that workers' engagement scores at Hyderabad were up 20% and that customer-centricity had risen significantly. In 2018 LinkedIn named the development center one of the top 25 places to work in India, and in 2019 it won a prestigious Zinnov Award as "a great place to innovate."

From "Innoganda" to Impact

Though the DBS story started with a call to action from its CEO, the work in Hyderabad operated several rungs lower in the organization. Indeed, one of the powerful things about BEANs is that they can be effective at the level of a team, a department, or a business unit, or companywide.

A few words of caution before our parting advice: Companies seeking to spark innovation often copy artifacts they see in other innovative companies. Maybe they install a well-stocked cafeteria with bright colors or provide scooters. But quick-and-easy artifacts that are bolted on and don't connect with day-to-day behaviors won't work.

One of us, Scott, observed an instance of this when he visited a socially oriented venture in Cambodia. It employs thousands of poor artisans, who create garments, carvings, statues, and more. One silkworm farm connected to the venture had put out a bright-blue box and invited workers to leave in it feedback and ideas "for you, for your colleagues, and for your well-being." Sounds inspirational, right?

There was just one problem. The rusted lock on the box betrayed that it hadn't been opened recently—or maybe ever. Such "innoganda"—innovation propaganda—just serves as a painful reminder of the things leadership is not doing. While it may generate a burst of energy at first, it will surely lead to cynicism over the long term.

Even the best BEAN can turn into innoganda without the right support—without (at the risk of torturing the metaphor) someone to tend the soil. When DBS began its journey, many employees, especially leaders, believed that innovation was the preserve of scientific and creative types. To counter that, a DBS team tasked with encouraging cultural change launched programs to teach employees how to innovate. For example, the team partnered with HR to create weeklong events in which executives got three days of training on digital concepts and then took part in a 48-hour "hackathon," joining people from real startups to create prototypes for apps solving real business problems. On the final afternoon the prototypes were pitched to the CEO.

Having executives experience the new mindset and behaviors the company wanted to promote helped make the programs it implemented practical, authentic, and organizationally consistent. Now, when DBS launches new BEANs, they're met not with eye rolls (or, worse, active resistance) but with game curiosity. As BEANs have taken root and proved their value in ways that directly benefit employees and the organization, they've been embraced.

If more and more companies methodically dismantle blockers to innovation and encourage employees to experiment, perhaps we will finally see the gap close between leaders' innovation goals and reality. Remember, when the people in your organization were children, they were brimming with curiosity and creativity. Your job is to bring that youthful spirit back to life.

Originally published in November–December 2019. Reprint R1906E

Leading Change

Why Transformation Efforts Fail. *by John P. Kotter*

OVER THE PAST DECADE, I have watched more than 100 companies try to remake themselves into significantly better competitors. They have included large organizations (Ford) and small ones (Landmark Communications), companies based in the United States (General Motors) and elsewhere (British Airways), corporations that were on their knees (Eastern Airlines), and companies that were earning good money (Bristol-Myers Squibb). These efforts have gone under many banners: total quality management, reengineering, rightsizing, restructuring, cultural change, and turnaround. But, in almost every case, the basic goal has been the same: to make fundamental changes in how business is conducted in order to help cope with a new, more challenging market environment.

A few of these corporate change efforts have been very successful. A few have been utter failures. Most fall somewhere in between, with a distinct tilt toward the lower end of the scale. The lessons that can be drawn are interesting and will probably be relevant to even more organizations in the increasingly competitive business environment of the coming decade.

The most general lesson to be learned from the more successful cases is that the change process goes through a series of phases that, in total, usually require a considerable length of time. Skipping steps creates only the illusion of speed and never produces a satisfying result. A second very general lesson is that critical mistakes in any of the phases can have a devastating impact, slowing momentum and negating hard-won gains. Perhaps because we have relatively little

Eight steps to transforming your organization

1. Establishing a sense of urgency
   - Examining market and competitive realities
   - Identifying and discussing crises, potential crises, or major opportunities

2. Forming a powerful guiding coalition
   - Assembling a group with enough power to lead the change effort
   - Encouraging the group to work together as a team

3. Creating a vision
   - Creating a vision to help direct the change effort
   - Developing strategies for achieving that vision

4. Communicating the vision
   - Using every vehicle possible to communicate the new vision and strategies
   - Teaching new behaviors by the example of the guiding coalition

5. Empowering others to act on the vision
   - Getting rid of obstacles to change
   - Changing systems or structures that seriously undermine the vision
   - Encouraging risk-taking and nontraditional ideas, activities, and actions

6. Planning for and creating short-term wins
   - Planning for visible performance improvements
   - Creating those improvements
   - Recognizing and rewarding employees involved in the improvements

7. Consolidating improvements and producing still more change
   - Using increased credibility to change systems, structures, and policies that don't fit the vision
   - Hiring, promoting, and developing employees who can implement the vision
   - Reinvigorating the process with new projects, themes, and change agents

8. Institutionalizing new approaches
   - Articulating the connections between the new behaviors and corporate success
   - Developing the means to ensure leadership development and succession

Idea in Brief

Most major change initiatives—whether intended to boost quality, improve culture, or reverse a corporate death spiral—generate only lukewarm results. Many fail miserably.

Why? Kotter maintains that too many leaders don't realize transformation is a *process*, not an event. It advances through stages that build on each other. And it takes years. Pressured to accelerate the process, leaders skip stages. But shortcuts never work.

Equally troubling, even highly capable leaders make critical mistakes—such as declaring victory too soon. Result? Loss of momentum, reversal of hard-won gains, and devastation of the entire transformation effort.

By understanding the stages of change—and the pitfalls unique to each stage—you boost your chances of a successful transformation. The payoff? Your organization flexes with tectonic shifts in competitors, markets, and technologies—leaving rivals far behind.

experience in renewing organizations, even very capable people often make at least one big error.

Error 1: Not Establishing a Great Enough Sense of Urgency

Most successful change efforts begin when some individuals or some groups start to look hard at a company's competitive situation, market position, technological trends, and financial performance. They focus on the potential revenue drop when an important patent expires, the five-year trend in declining margins in a core business, or an emerging market that everyone seems to be ignoring. They then find ways to communicate this information broadly and dramatically, especially with respect to crises, potential crises, or great opportunities that are very timely. This first step is essential because just getting a transformation program started requires the aggressive cooperation of many individuals. Without motivation, people won't help, and the effort goes nowhere.

Compared with other steps in the change process, phase one can sound easy. It is not. Well over 50% of the companies I have

Idea in Practice

To give your transformation effort the best chance of succeeding, take the right actions at each stage—and avoid common pitfalls.

Stage	Actions needed	Pitfalls
Establish a sense of urgency	• Examine market and competitive realities for potential crises and untapped opportunities. • Convince at least 75% of your managers that the status quo is more dangerous than the unknown.	• Underestimating the difficulty of driving people from their comfort zones • Becoming paralyzed by risks
Form a powerful guiding coalition	• Assemble a group with shared commitment and enough power to lead the change effort. • Encourage them to work as a team outside the normal hierarchy.	• No prior experience in teamwork at the top • Relegating team leadership to an HR, quality, or strategic-planning executive rather than a senior line manager
Create a vision	• Create a vision to direct the change effort. • Develop strategies for realizing that vision.	• Presenting a vision that is too complicated or vague to be communicated in five minutes
Communicate the vision	• Use every vehicle possible to communicate the new vision and strategies for achieving it. • Teach new behaviors by the example of the guiding coalition.	• Undercommunicating the vision • Behaving in ways antithetical to the vision

watched fail in this first phase. What are the reasons for that failure? Sometimes executives underestimate how hard it can be to drive people out of their comfort zones. Sometimes they grossly overestimate how successful they have already been in increasing urgency. Sometimes they lack patience: "Enough with the preliminaries; let's get on with it." In many cases, executives become paralyzed by the downside possibilities. They worry that

Empower others to act on the vision	• Remove or alter systems or structures undermining the vision. • Encourage risk-taking and nontraditional ideas, activities, and actions.	• Failing to remove powerful individuals who resist the change effort
Plan for and create short-term wins	• Define and engineer visible performance improvements. • Recognize and reward employees contributing to those improvements.	• Leaving short-term successes up to chance • Failing to score successes early enough (12–24 months into the change effort)
Consolidate improvements and produce more change	• Use increased credibility from early wins to change systems, structures, and policies undermining the vision. • Hire, promote, and develop employees who can implement the vision. • Reinvigorate the change process with new projects and change agents.	• Declaring victory too soon—with the first performance improvement • Allowing resisters to convince "troops" that the war has been won
Institutionalize new approaches	• Articulate connections between new behaviors and corporate success. • Create leadership development and succession plans consistent with the new approach.	• Not creating new social norms and shared values consistent with changes • Promoting people who don't personify the new approach into leadership positions

employees with seniority will become defensive, that morale will drop, that events will spin out of control, that short-term business results will be jeopardized, that the stock will sink, and that they will be blamed for creating a crisis.

A paralyzed senior management often comes from having too many managers and not enough leaders. Management's mandate is to minimize risk and to keep the current system operating. Change, by definition, requires creating a new system, which in turn always demands leadership. Phase one in a renewal process typically goes nowhere until enough real leaders are promoted or hired into senior-level jobs.

Transformations often begin, and begin well, when an organization has a new head who is a good leader and who sees the need for a major change. If the renewal target is the entire company, the CEO is key. If change is needed in a division, the division general manager is key. When these individuals are not new leaders, great leaders, or change champions, phase one can be a huge challenge.

Bad business results are both a blessing and a curse in the first phase. On the positive side, losing money does catch people's attention. But it also gives less maneuvering room. With good business results, the opposite is true: Convincing people of the need for change is much harder, but you have more resources to help make changes.

But whether the starting point is good performance or bad, in the more successful cases I have witnessed, an individual or a group always facilitates a frank discussion of potentially unpleasant facts about new competition, shrinking margins, decreasing market share, flat earnings, a lack of revenue growth, or other relevant indices of a declining competitive position. Because there seems to be an almost universal human tendency to shoot the bearer of bad news, especially if the head of the organization is not a change champion, executives in these companies often rely on outsiders to bring unwanted information. Wall Street analysts, customers, and consultants can all be helpful in this regard. The purpose of all this activity, in the words of one former CEO of a large European company, is "to make the status quo seem more dangerous than launching into the unknown."

In a few of the most successful cases, a group has manufactured a crisis. One CEO deliberately engineered the largest accounting loss in the company's history, creating huge pressures from Wall Street in the process. One division president commissioned first-ever customer satisfaction surveys, knowing full well that the results would be terrible. He then made these findings public. On the surface, such moves can look unduly risky. But there is also risk in playing it too safe: When the urgency rate is not pumped up enough, the transformation process cannot succeed, and the long-term future of the organization is put in jeopardy.

When is the urgency rate high enough? From what I have seen, the answer is when about 75% of a company's management is honestly convinced that business as usual is totally unacceptable. Anything less can produce very serious problems later on in the process.

Error 2: Not Creating a Powerful Enough Guiding Coalition

Major renewal programs often start with just one or two people. In cases of successful transformation efforts, the leadership coalition grows and grows over time. But whenever some minimum mass is not achieved early in the effort, nothing much worthwhile happens.

It is often said that major change is impossible unless the head of the organization is an active supporter. What I am talking about goes far beyond that. In successful transformations, the chairman or president or division general manager, plus another five or 15 or 50 people, come together and develop a shared commitment to excellent performance through renewal. In my experience, this group never includes all of the company's most senior executives because some people just won't buy in, at least not at first. But in the most successful cases, the coalition is always pretty powerful— in terms of titles, information and expertise, reputations, and relationships.

In both small and large organizations, a successful guiding team may consist of only three to five people during the first year of a renewal effort. But in big companies, the coalition needs to grow to the 20 to 50 range before much progress can be made in phase three and beyond. Senior managers always form the core of the group. But sometimes you find board members, a representative from a key customer, or even a powerful union leader.

Because the guiding coalition includes members who are not part of senior management, it tends to operate outside of the normal hierarchy by definition. This can be awkward, but it is clearly necessary. If the existing hierarchy were working well, there would be no need for a major transformation. But since the current system is not working, reform generally demands activity outside of formal boundaries, expectations, and protocol.

A high sense of urgency within the managerial ranks helps enormously in putting a guiding coalition together. But more is usually required. Someone needs to get these people together, help them develop a shared assessment of their company's problems and opportunities, and create a minimum level of trust and communication. Off-site retreats, for two or three days, are one popular vehicle for accomplishing this task. I have seen many groups of five to 35 executives attend a series of these retreats over a period of months.

Companies that fail in phase two usually underestimate the difficulties of producing change and thus the importance of a powerful guiding coalition. Sometimes they have no history of teamwork at the top and therefore undervalue the importance of this type of coalition. Sometimes they expect the team to be led by a staff executive from human resources, quality, or strategic planning instead of a key line manager. No matter how capable or dedicated the staff head, groups without strong line leadership never achieve the power that is required.

Efforts that don't have a powerful enough guiding coalition can make apparent progress for a while. But, sooner or later, the opposition gathers itself together and stops the change.

Error 3: Lacking a Vision

In every successful transformation effort that I have seen, the guiding coalition develops a picture of the future that is relatively easy to communicate and appeals to customers, stockholders, and employees. A vision always goes beyond the numbers that are typically found in five-year plans. A vision says something that helps clarify the direction in which an organization needs to move. Sometimes the first draft comes mostly from a single individual. It is usually a bit blurry, at least initially. But after the coalition works at it for three or five or even 12 months, something much better emerges through their tough analytical thinking and a little dreaming. Eventually, a strategy for achieving that vision is also developed.

In one midsize European company, the first pass at a vision contained two-thirds of the basic ideas that were in the final product. The concept of global reach was in the initial version from the beginning. So was the idea of becoming preeminent in certain businesses. But one central idea in the final version—getting out of low value-added activities—came only after a series of discussions over a period of several months.

Without a sensible vision, a transformation effort can easily dissolve into a list of confusing and incompatible projects that can take the organization in the wrong direction or nowhere at all. Without a sound vision, the reengineering project in the accounting department, the new 360-degree performance appraisal from the human resources department, the plant's quality program, and the cultural change project in the sales force will not add up in a meaningful way.

In failed transformations, you often find plenty of plans, directives, and programs but no vision. In one case, a company gave out four-inch-thick notebooks describing its change effort. In mind-numbing detail, the books spelled out procedures, goals, methods, and deadlines. But nowhere was there a clear and compelling statement of where all this was leading. Not surprisingly, most of the employees with whom I talked were either confused or alienated. The big, thick books did not rally them together or inspire change. In fact, they probably had just the opposite effect.

In a few of the less successful cases that I have seen, management had a sense of direction, but it was too complicated or blurry to be useful. Recently, I asked an executive in a midsize company to describe his vision and received in return a barely comprehensible 30-minute lecture. Buried in his answer were the basic elements of a sound vision. But they were buried—deeply.

A useful rule of thumb: If you can't communicate the vision to someone in five minutes or less and get a reaction that signifies both understanding and interest, you are not yet done with this phase of the transformation process.

Error 4: Undercommunicating the Vision by a Factor of 10

I've seen three patterns with respect to communication, all very common. In the first, a group actually does develop a pretty good transformation vision and then proceeds to communicate it by holding a single meeting or sending out a single communication. Having used about 0.0001% of the yearly intracompany communication, the group is startled when few people seem to understand the new approach. In the second pattern, the head of the organization spends a considerable amount of time making speeches to employee groups, but most people still don't get it (not surprising, since vision captures only 0.0005% of the total yearly communication). In the third pattern, much more effort goes into newsletters and speeches, but some very visible senior executives still behave in ways that are antithetical to the vision. The net result is that cynicism among the troops goes up, while belief in the communication goes down.

Transformation is impossible unless hundreds or thousands of people are willing to help, often to the point of making short-term sacrifices. Employees will not make sacrifices, even if they are unhappy with the status quo, unless they believe that useful change is possible. Without credible communication, and a lot of it, the hearts and minds of the troops are never captured.

This fourth phase is particularly challenging if the short-term sacrifices include job losses. Gaining understanding and support is tough when downsizing is a part of the vision. For this reason, successful visions usually include new growth possibilities and the commitment to treat fairly anyone who is laid off.

Executives who communicate well incorporate messages into their hour-by-hour activities. In a routine discussion about a business problem, they talk about how proposed solutions fit (or don't fit) into the bigger picture. In a regular performance appraisal, they talk about how the employee's behavior helps or undermines the vision. In a review of a division's quarterly performance, they talk not only about the numbers but also about how the division's executives are contributing to the transformation. In a routine Q&A with employees at a company facility, they tie their answers back to renewal goals.

In more successful transformation efforts, executives use all existing communication channels to broadcast the vision. They turn boring, unread company newsletters into lively articles about the vision. They take ritualistic, tedious quarterly management meetings and turn them into exciting discussions of the transformation. They throw out much of the company's generic management education and replace it with courses that focus on business problems and the new vision. The guiding principle is simple: Use every possible channel, especially those that are being wasted on nonessential information.

Perhaps even more important, most of the executives I have known in successful cases of major change learn to "walk the talk." They consciously attempt to become a living symbol of the new corporate culture. This is often not easy. A 60-year-old plant manager who has spent precious little time over 40 years thinking about customers will not suddenly behave in a customer-oriented way. But I have witnessed just such a person change, and change a great deal. In that case, a high level of urgency helped. The fact that the man was a part of the guiding coalition and the vision-creation team also helped. So did all the communication, which kept reminding him of the desired behavior, and all the feedback from his peers and subordinates, which helped him see when he was not engaging in that behavior.

Communication comes in both words and deeds, and the latter are often the most powerful form. Nothing undermines change more than behavior by important individuals that is inconsistent with their words.

Error 5: Not Removing Obstacles to the New Vision

Successful transformations begin to involve large numbers of people as the process progresses. Employees are emboldened to try new approaches, to develop new ideas, and to provide leadership. The only constraint is that the actions fit within the broad parameters of the overall vision. The more people involved, the better the outcome.

To some degree, a guiding coalition empowers others to take action simply by successfully communicating the new direction. But communication is never sufficient by itself. Renewal also requires the removal of obstacles. Too often, an employee understands the new vision and wants to help make it happen, but an elephant appears to be blocking the path. In some cases, the elephant is in the person's head, and the challenge is to convince the individual that no external obstacle exists. But in most cases, the blockers are very real.

Sometimes the obstacle is the organizational structure: Narrow job categories can seriously undermine efforts to increase productivity or make it very difficult even to think about customers. Sometimes compensation or performance-appraisal systems make people choose between the new vision and their own self-interest. Perhaps worst of all are bosses who refuse to change and who make demands that are inconsistent with the overall effort.

One company began its transformation process with much publicity and actually made good progress through the fourth phase. Then the change effort ground to a halt because the officer in charge of the company's largest division was allowed to undermine most of the new initiatives. He paid lip service to the process but did not change his behavior or encourage his managers to change. He did not reward the unconventional ideas called for in the vision. He allowed human resource systems to remain intact even when they were clearly inconsistent with the new ideals. I think the officer's motives were complex. To some degree, he did not believe the company needed major change. To some degree, he felt personally threatened by all the change. To some degree, he was afraid that he could not produce both change and the expected operating profit. But despite the fact that they backed the renewal effort, the other officers did virtually nothing to stop the one blocker. Again, the reasons were complex. The company had no history of confronting problems like this. Some people were afraid of the officer. The CEO was concerned that he might lose a talented executive. The net result was disastrous. Lower-level managers concluded that senior management had lied to them about their commitment to renewal, cynicism grew, and the whole effort collapsed.

In the first half of a transformation, no organization has the momentum, power, or time to get rid of all obstacles. But the big ones must be confronted and removed. If the blocker is a person, it is important that he or she be treated fairly and in a way that is consistent with the new vision. Action is essential, both to empower others and to maintain the credibility of the change effort as a whole.

Error 6: Not Systematically Planning for, and Creating, Short-Term Wins

Real transformation takes time, and a renewal effort risks losing momentum if there are no short-term goals to meet and celebrate. Most people won't go on the long march unless they see compelling evidence in 12 to 24 months that the journey is producing expected results. Without short-term wins, too many people give up or actively join the ranks of those people who have been resisting change.

One to two years into a successful transformation effort, you find quality beginning to go up on certain indices or the decline in net income stopping. You find some successful new product introductions or an upward shift in market share. You find an impressive productivity improvement or a statistically higher customer satisfaction rating. But whatever the case, the win is unambiguous. The result is not just a judgment call that can be discounted by those opposing change.

Creating short-term wins is different from hoping for short-term wins. The latter is passive, the former active. In a successful transformation, managers actively look for ways to obtain clear performance improvements, establish goals in the yearly planning system, achieve the objectives, and reward the people involved with recognition, promotions, and even money. For example, the guiding coalition at a U.S. manufacturing company produced a highly visible and successful new product introduction about 20 months after the start of its renewal effort. The new product was selected about six months into the effort because it met multiple criteria: It could be designed and launched in a relatively short period, it could be handled by a small team of people who were devoted to the new vision, it had upside potential, and the new product-development team could operate outside the established departmental structure without practical problems. Little was left to chance, and the win boosted the credibility of the renewal process.

Managers often complain about being forced to produce short-term wins, but I've found that pressure can be a useful element in a change effort. When it becomes clear to people that major change will take a long time, urgency levels can drop. Commitments to produce short-term wins help keep the urgency level up and force detailed analytical thinking that can clarify or revise visions.

Error 7: Declaring Victory Too Soon

After a few years of hard work, managers may be tempted to declare victory with the first clear performance improvement. While celebrating a win is fine, declaring the war won can be catastrophic. Until changes sink deeply into a company's culture, a process that can take five to 10 years, new approaches are fragile and subject to regression.

In the recent past, I have watched a dozen change efforts operate under the reengineering theme. In all but two cases, victory was declared and the expensive consultants were paid and thanked when the first major project was completed after two to three years. Within two more years, the useful changes that had been introduced slowly disappeared. In two of the 10 cases, it's hard to find any trace of the reengineering work today.

Over the past 20 years, I've seen the same sort of thing happen to huge quality projects, organizational development efforts, and more. Typically, the problems start early in the process: The urgency level is not intense enough, the guiding coalition is not powerful enough, and the vision is not clear enough. But it is the premature victory celebration that kills momentum. And then the powerful forces associated with tradition take over.

Ironically, it is often a combination of change initiators and change resisters that creates the premature victory celebration. In their enthusiasm over a clear sign of progress, the initiators go overboard. They are then joined by resisters, who are quick to spot any opportunity to stop change. After the celebration is over, the resisters point to the victory as a sign that the war has been won and the troops should be sent home. Weary troops allow themselves to be convinced that they won. Once home, the foot soldiers are reluctant to climb back on the ships. Soon thereafter, change comes to a halt, and tradition creeps back in.

Instead of declaring victory, leaders of successful efforts use the credibility afforded by short-term wins to tackle even bigger problems. They go after systems and structures that are not consistent with the transformation vision and have not been confronted before. They pay great attention to who is promoted, who is hired, and how people are developed. They include new reengineering projects that are even bigger in scope than the initial ones. They understand that renewal efforts take not months but years. In fact, in one of the most successful transformations that I have ever seen, we quantified the amount of change that occurred each year over a seven-year period. On a scale of 1 (low) to 10 (high), year one received a 2, year two a 4, year three a 3, year four a 7, year five an 8, year six a 4, and year seven a 2. The peak came in year five, fully 36 months after the first set of visible wins.

Error 8: Not Anchoring Changes in the Corporation's Culture

In the final analysis, change sticks when it becomes "the way we do things around here," when it seeps into the bloodstream of the corporate body. Until new behaviors are rooted in social norms and shared values, they are subject to degradation as soon as the pressure for change is removed.

Two factors are particularly important in institutionalizing change in corporate culture. The first is a conscious attempt to show people how the new approaches, behaviors, and attitudes have helped improve performance. When people are left on their own to make the connections, they sometimes create very inaccurate links. For example, because results improved while charismatic Harry was boss, the troops link his mostly idiosyncratic style with those results instead of seeing how their own improved customer service and productivity were instrumental. Helping people see the right connections requires communication. Indeed, one company was relentless, and it paid off enormously. Time was spent at every major management meeting to discuss why performance was increasing. The company newspaper ran article after article showing how changes had boosted earnings.

The second factor is taking sufficient time to make sure that the next generation of top management really does personify the new approach. If the requirements for promotion don't change, renewal rarely lasts. One bad succession decision at the top of an organization can undermine a decade of hard work. Poor succession decisions are possible when boards of directors are not an integral part of the renewal effort. In at least three instances I have seen, the champion for change was the retiring executive, and although his successor was not a resister, he was not a change champion. Because the boards did not understand the transformations in any detail, they could not see that their choices were not good fits. The retiring executive in one case tried unsuccessfully to talk his board into a less seasoned candidate who better personified the transformation. In the other two cases, the CEOs did not resist the boards' choices, because they felt the transformation could not be undone by their successors. They were wrong. Within two years, signs of renewal began to disappear at both companies.

———

There are still more mistakes that people make, but these eight are the big ones. I realize that in a short article everything is made to sound a bit too simplistic. In reality, even successful change efforts are messy and full of surprises. But just as a relatively simple vision is needed to guide people through a major change, so a vision of the change process can reduce the error rate. And fewer errors can spell the difference between success and failure.

Originally published in March 1995. Reprint R0701J

The Leader's Guide to Corporate Culture

by Boris Groysberg, Jeremiah Lee, Jesse Price, and J. Yo-Jud Cheng

STRATEGY AND CULTURE ARE AMONG the primary levers at top leaders' disposal in their never-ending quest to maintain organizational viability and effectiveness. Strategy offers a formal logic for the company's goals and orients people around them. Culture expresses goals through values and beliefs and guides activity through shared assumptions and group norms.

Strategy provides clarity and focus for collective action and decision-making. It relies on plans and sets of choices to mobilize people and can often be enforced by both concrete rewards for achieving goals and consequences for failing to do so. Ideally, it also incorporates adaptive elements that can scan and analyze the external environment and sense when changes are required to maintain continuity and growth. Leadership goes hand-in-hand with strategy formation, and most leaders understand the fundamentals. Culture, however, is a more elusive lever, because much of it is anchored in unspoken behaviors, mindsets, and social patterns.

For better *and* worse, culture and leadership are inextricably linked. Founders and influential leaders often set new cultures in motion and imprint values and assumptions that persist for decades. Over time an organization's leaders can also shape culture, through both conscious and unconscious actions (sometimes with unintended consequences). The best leaders we have observed are fully aware of the multiple cultures within which they are embedded, can sense when change is required, and can deftly influence the process.

Unfortunately, in our experience it is far more common for leaders seeking to build high-performing organizations to be confounded by culture. Indeed, many either let it go unmanaged or relegate it to the HR function, where it becomes a secondary concern for the business. They may lay out detailed, thoughtful plans for strategy and execution, but because they don't understand culture's power and dynamics, their plans go off the rails. As someone once said, culture eats strategy for breakfast.

It doesn't have to be that way. Our work suggests that culture can, in fact, be managed. The first and most important step leaders can take to maximize its value and minimize its risks is to become fully aware of how it works. By integrating findings from more than 100 of the most commonly used social and behavioral models, we have identified eight styles that distinguish a culture and can be measured. (We gratefully acknowledge the rich history of cultural studies—going all the way back to the earliest explorations of human nature—on which our work builds.) Using this framework, leaders can model the impact of culture on their business and assess its alignment with strategy. We also suggest how culture can help them achieve change and build organizations that thrive in even the most trying times.

Defining Culture

Culture is the tacit social order of an organization: It shapes attitudes and behaviors in wide-ranging and durable ways. Cultural norms define what is encouraged, discouraged, accepted, or rejected within a group. When properly aligned with personal values, drives, and needs, culture can unleash tremendous amounts of energy toward a shared purpose and foster an organization's capacity to thrive.

Culture can also evolve flexibly and autonomously in response to changing opportunities and demands. Whereas strategy is typically determined by the C-suite, culture can fluidly blend the

Idea in Brief

Executives are often confounded by culture, because much of it is anchored in unspoken behaviors, mindsets, and social patterns. Many leaders either let it go unmanaged or relegate it to HR, where it becomes a secondary concern for the business. This is a mistake, because properly managed, culture can help them achieve change and build organizations that will thrive in even the most trying times.

The authors have reviewed the literature on culture and distilled eight distinct culture styles: *caring*, focused on relationships and mutual trust; *purpose*, exemplified by idealism and altruism; *learning*, characterized by exploration, expansiveness, and creativity; *enjoyment*, expressed through fun and excitement; *results*, characterized by achievement and winning; *authority*, defined by strength, decisiveness, and boldness; *safety*, defined by planning, caution, and preparedness; and *order*, focused on respect, structure, and shared norms.

These eight styles fit into an "integrated culture framework"

according to the degree to which they reflect independence or interdependence (people interactions) and flexibility or stability (response to change). They can be used to diagnose and describe highly complex and diverse behavioral patterns in a culture and to model how likely an individual leader is to align with and shape that culture.

Through research and practical experience, the authors have arrived at five insights regarding culture's effect on companies' success: (1) When aligned with strategy and leadership, a strong culture drives positive organizational outcomes. (2) Selecting or developing leaders for the future requires a forward-looking strategy and culture. (3) In a merger, designing a new culture on the basis of complementary strengths can speed up integration and create more value over time. (4) In a dynamic, uncertain environment, in which organizations must be more agile, learning gains importance. (5) A strong culture can be a significant liability when it is misaligned with strategy.

intentions of top leaders with the knowledge and experiences of frontline employees.

The academic literature on the subject is vast. Our review of it revealed many formal definitions of organizational culture and a variety of models and methods for assessing it. Numerous processes exist for creating and changing it. Agreement on specifics is sparse across these definitions, models, and methods, but through a synthesis of seminal work by Edgar Schein, Shalom Schwartz, Geert Hofstede, and other leading scholars, we have identified four generally accepted attributes:

Shared

Culture is a group phenomenon. It cannot exist solely within a single person, nor is it simply the average of individual characteristics. It resides in shared behaviors, values, and assumptions and is most commonly experienced through the norms and expectations of a group—that is, the unwritten rules.

Pervasive

Culture permeates multiple levels and applies very broadly in an organization; sometimes it is even conflated with the organization itself. It is manifest in collective behaviors, physical environments, group rituals, visible symbols, stories, and legends. Other aspects of culture are unseen, such as mindsets, motivations, unspoken assumptions, and what David Rooke and William Torbert refer to as "action logics" (mental models of how to interpret and respond to the world around you).

Enduring

Culture can direct the thoughts and actions of group members over the long term. It develops through critical events in the collective life and learning of a group. Its endurance is explained in part by the attraction-selection-attrition model first introduced by Benjamin Schneider: People are drawn to organizations with characteristics similar to their own; organizations are more likely to select individuals who seem to "fit in"; and over time those who don't fit in tend to leave. Thus culture becomes a self-reinforcing social pattern that grows increasingly resistant to change and outside influences.

Implicit

An important and often overlooked aspect of culture is that despite its subliminal nature, people are effectively hardwired to recognize and respond to it instinctively. It acts as a kind of silent language. Shalom

Schwartz and E. O. Wilson have shown through their research how evolutionary processes shaped human capacity; because the ability to sense and respond to culture is universal, certain themes should be expected to recur across the many models, definitions, and studies in the field. That is exactly what we have discovered in our research over the past few decades.

Eight Distinct Culture Styles

Our review of the literature for commonalities and central concepts revealed two primary dimensions that apply regardless of organization type, size, industry, or geography: people interactions and response to change. Understanding a company's culture requires determining where it falls along these two dimensions.

People interactions

An organization's orientation toward people interactions and coordination will fall on a spectrum from highly independent to highly interdependent. Cultures that lean toward the former place greater value on autonomy, individual action, and competition. Those that lean toward the latter emphasize integration, managing relationships, and coordinating group effort. People in such cultures tend to collaborate and to see success through the lens of the group.

Response to change

Whereas some cultures emphasize stability—prioritizing consistency, predictability, and maintenance of the status quo—others emphasize flexibility, adaptability, and receptiveness to change. Those that favor stability tend to follow rules, use control structures such as seniority-based staffing, reinforce hierarchy, and strive for efficiency. Those that favor flexibility tend to prioritize innovation, openness, diversity, and a longer-term orientation. (Kim Cameron, Robert Quinn, and Robert Ernest are among the researchers who employ similar dimensions in their culture frameworks.)

By applying this fundamental insight about the dimensions of people interactions and response to change, we have identified eight styles that apply to both organizational cultures and individual leaders. Researchers at Spencer Stuart (including two of this article's authors) have interdependently studied and refined this list of styles across both levels over the past two decades.

Caring focuses on relationships and mutual trust. Work environments are warm, collaborative, and welcoming places where people help and support one another. Employees are united by loyalty; leaders emphasize sincerity, teamwork, and positive relationships.

Purpose is exemplified by idealism and altruism. Work environments are tolerant, compassionate places where people try to do good for the long-term future of the world. Employees are united by a focus on sustainability and global communities; leaders emphasize shared ideals and contributing to a greater cause.

Learning is characterized by exploration, expansiveness, and creativity. Work environments are inventive and open-minded places where people spark new ideas and explore alternatives. Employees are united by curiosity; leaders emphasize innovation, knowledge, and adventure.

Enjoyment is expressed through fun and excitement. Work environments are lighthearted places where people tend to do what makes them happy. Employees are united by playfulness and stimulation; leaders emphasize spontaneity and a sense of humor.

Results is characterized by achievement and winning. Work environments are outcome-oriented and merit-based places where people aspire to achieve top performance. Employees are united by a drive for capability and success; leaders emphasize goal accomplishment.

Authority is defined by strength, decisiveness, and boldness. Work environments are competitive places where people strive to gain personal advantage. Employees are united by strong control; leaders emphasize confidence and dominance.

Safety is defined by planning, caution, and preparedness. Work environments are predictable places where people are risk-conscious and think things through carefully. Employees are united by a desire to feel protected and anticipate change; leaders emphasize being realistic and planning ahead.

Order is focused on respect, structure, and shared norms. Work environments are methodical places where people tend to play by the rules and want to fit in. Employees are united by cooperation; leaders emphasize shared procedures and time-honored customs.

These eight styles fit into our integrated culture framework (see the exhibit "Integrated culture: The framework") according to the degree to which they reflect independence or interdependence (people interactions) and flexibility or stability (response to change). Styles that are adjacent in the framework, such as *safety* and *order,* frequently coexist within organizations and their people. In contrast, styles that are located across from each other, such as *safety* and *learning,* are less likely to be found together and require more organizational energy to maintain simultaneously. Each style has advantages and disadvantages, and no style is inherently better than another. An organizational culture can be defined by the absolute and relative strengths of each of the eight and by the degree of employee agreement about which styles characterize the organization. A powerful feature of this framework, which differentiates it from other models, is that it can also be used to define individuals' styles and the values of leaders and employees.

Inherent in the framework are fundamental trade-offs. Although each style can be beneficial, natural constraints and competing demands force difficult choices about which values to emphasize and how people are expected to behave. It is common to find organizations with cultures that emphasize both *results* and *caring,* but this combination can be confusing to employees. Are they expected to optimize individual goals and strive for outcomes at all costs, or should they work as a team and emphasize collaboration and shared success? The nature of the work itself, the business strategy, or the design of the organization may make it difficult for employees to be equally *results* focused and *caring.*

In contrast, a culture that emphasizes *caring* and *order* encourages a work environment in which teamwork, trust, and respect are paramount. The two styles are mutually reinforcing, which can be beneficial but can also present challenges. The benefits are strong loyalty, retention of talent, lack of conflict, and high levels of engagement.

Integrated culture: The framework

On the basis of decades of experience analyzing organizations, executives, and employees, we developed a rigorous, comprehensive model to identify the key attributes of both group culture and individual leadership styles. Eight characteristics emerge when we map cultures along two dimensions: how people interact (independence to interdependence) and their response to change (flexibility to stability). The relative salience of these eight styles differs across organizations, though nearly all are strongly characterized by **results** *and* **caring.**

The spatial relationships are important. Proximate styles, such as **safety** *and* **order,** *or* **learning** *and* **enjoyment,** *will coexist more easily than styles that are far apart on the chart, such as* **authority** *and* **purpose,** *or* **safety** *and* **learning.** *Achieving a culture of* **authority** *often means gaining the advantages (and living with the disadvantages) of that culture but missing out on the advantages (and avoiding the disadvantages) of a culture of* **purpose.**

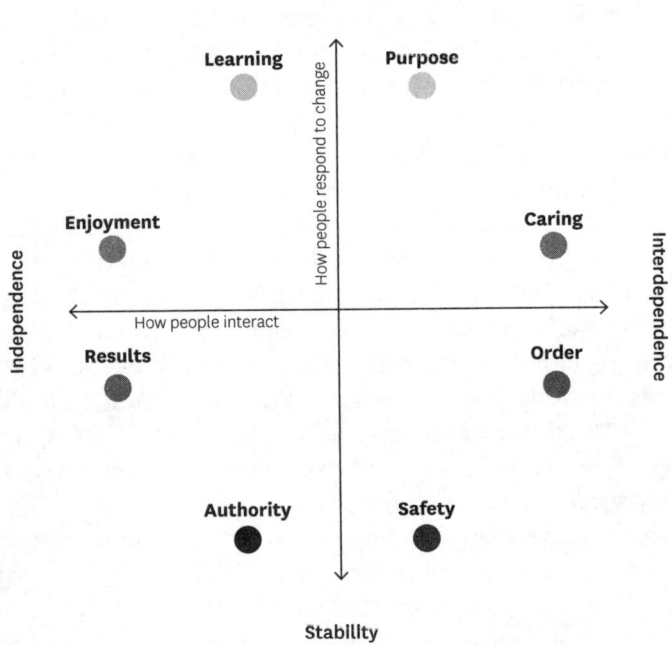

Source: Spencer Stuart.

Integrated culture: Leader statements

Top leaders and founders often express cultural sentiments within the public domain, either intentionally or unintentionally. Such statements can provide important clues to how these leaders are thinking about and leading their organizations' cultures.

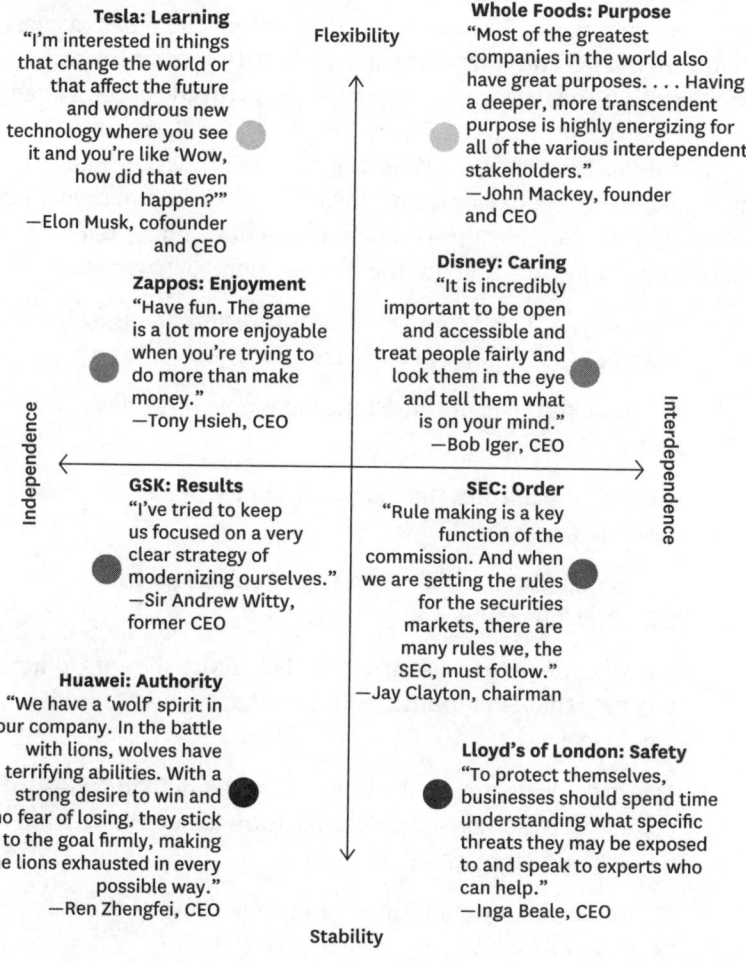

Tesla: Learning
"I'm interested in things that change the world or that affect the future and wondrous new technology where you see it and you're like 'Wow, how did that even happen?'"
—Elon Musk, cofounder and CEO

Flexibility

Whole Foods: Purpose
"Most of the greatest companies in the world also have great purposes. . . . Having a deeper, more transcendent purpose is highly energizing for all of the various interdependent stakeholders."
—John Mackey, founder and CEO

Zappos: Enjoyment
"Have fun. The game is a lot more enjoyable when you're trying to do more than make money."
—Tony Hsieh, CEO

Disney: Caring
"It is incredibly important to be open and accessible and treat people fairly and look them in the eye and tell them what is on your mind."
—Bob Iger, CEO

Independence

Interdependence

GSK: Results
"I've tried to keep us focused on a very clear strategy of modernizing ourselves."
—Sir Andrew Witty, former CEO

SEC: Order
"Rule making is a key function of the commission. And when we are setting the rules for the securities markets, there are many rules we, the SEC, must follow."
—Jay Clayton, chairman

Huawei: Authority
"We have a 'wolf' spirit in our company. In the battle with lions, wolves have terrifying abilities. With a strong desire to win and no fear of losing, they stick to the goal firmly, making the lions exhausted in every possible way."
—Ren Zhengfei, CEO

Lloyd's of London: Safety
"To protect themselves, businesses should spend time understanding what specific threats they may be exposed to and speak to experts who can help."
—Inga Beale, CEO

Stability

The challenges are a tendency toward groupthink, reliance on consensus-based decisions, avoidance of difficult issues, and a calcified sense of "us versus them." Leaders who are more focused on *results* and *learning* may find the combination of *caring* and *order* stifling when they seek to drive entrepreneurship and change. Savvy leaders make use of existing cultural strengths and have a nuanced understanding of how to initiate change. They might rely on the participative nature of a culture focused on *caring* and *order* to engage team members and simultaneously identify a *learning*-oriented "insider" who has the trust of his or her peers to advocate for change through relationship networks.

The eight styles can be used to diagnose and describe highly complex and diverse behavioral patterns in a culture and to model how likely an individual leader is to align with and shape that culture. Using this framework and multilevel approach, managers can:

- Understand their organization's culture and assess its intended and unintended effects

- Evaluate the level of consistency in employees' views of the culture

- Identify subcultures that may account for higher or lower group performance

- Pinpoint differences between legacy cultures during mergers and acquisitions

- Rapidly orient new executives to the culture they are joining and help them determine the most effective way to lead employees

- Measure the degree of alignment between individual leadership styles and organizational culture to determine what impact a leader might have

- Design an aspirational culture and communicate the changes necessary to achieve it

The Link Between Culture and Outcomes

Our research and practical experience have shown that when you are evaluating how culture affects outcomes, the context in which the organization operates—geographic region, industry, strategy, leadership, and company structure—matters, as does the strength of the culture. (See "Context, Conditions, and Culture," the sidebar at the end of this article.) What worked in the past may no longer work in the future, and what worked for one company may not work for another.

We have arrived at the following insights:

When aligned with strategy and leadership, a strong culture drives positive organizational outcomes

Consider the case of a best-in-class retailer headquartered in the United States. The company had viewed its first priority as providing top-notch customer service. It accomplished this with a simple rule—Do right by the customer—that encouraged employees to use their judgment when providing service. A core HR training practice was to help every salesperson see customer interactions as an opportunity to create "service stories that become legendary." Employees were reminded to define service from the customer's perspective, to constantly engage customers with questions geared toward understanding their specific needs and preferences, and to go beyond their expectations.

In measuring the culture of this company, we found that like many other large retailers, it was characterized primarily by a combination of *results* and *caring*. Unlike many other retailers, however, it had a culture that was also very flexible, *learning* oriented, and focused on *purpose*. As one top executive explained, "We have freedom as long as we take good care of the customer."

Furthermore, the company's values and norms were very clear to everyone and consistently shared throughout the organization. As the retailer expanded into new segments and geographies over the years, the leadership strove to maintain an intense customer focus

The pros and cons of culture styles

Every culture style has strengths and weaknesses. The table below summarizes the advantages and disadvantages of each style and how frequently it appears as a defining culture characteristic among the companies in our study.

Culture style	Advantages	Disadvantages	Ranked 1st or 2nd
Caring Warm, sincere, relational	Improved teamwork, engagement, communication, trust, and sense of belonging	Overemphasis on consensus building may reduce exploration of options, stifle competitiveness, and slow decision-making	63%
Purpose Purpose-driven, idealistic, tolerant	Improved appreciation for diversity, sustainability, and social responsibility	Overemphasis on a long-term purpose and ideals may get in the way of practical and immediate concerns	9%
Learning Open, inventive, exploring	Improved innovation, agility, and organizational learning	Overemphasis on exploration may lead to a lack of focus and an inability to exploit existing advantages	7%
Enjoyment Playful, instinctive, fun-loving	Improved employee morale, engagement, and creativity	Overemphasis on autonomy and engagement may lead to a lack of discipline and create possible compliance or governance issues	2%
Results Achievement-driven, goal-focused	Improved execution, external focus, capability building, and goal achievement	Overemphasis on achieving results may lead to communication and collaboration breakdowns and higher levels of stress and anxiety	89%

Authority Bold, decisive, dominant	Improved speed of decision-making and responsiveness to threats or crises	Overemphasis on strong authority and bold decision-making may lead to politics, conflict, and a psychologically unsafe work environment	4%
Safety Realistic, careful, prepared	Improved risk management, stability, and business continuity	Overemphasis on standardization and formalization may lead to bureaucracy, inflexibility, and dehumanization of the work environment	8%
Order Rule-abiding, respectful, cooperative	Improved operational efficiency, reduced conflict, and greater civic-mindedness	Overemphasis on rules and traditions may reduce individualism, stifle creativity, and limit organizational agility	15%

Note: Sum of percentages is greater than 100 because styles were counted as dominant if they were ranked 1 or 2 overall.

without diluting its cherished culture. Although the company had historically focused on developing leaders from within—who were natural culture carriers—recruiting outsiders became necessary as it grew. The company preserved its culture through this change by carefully assessing new leaders and designing an onboarding process that reinforced core values and norms.

Culture is a powerful differentiator for this company because it is strongly aligned with strategy and leadership. Delivering outstanding customer service requires a culture and a mindset that emphasize achievement, impeccable service, and problem-solving through autonomy and inventiveness. Not surprisingly, those qualities have led to a variety of positive outcomes for the company, including robust growth and international expansion, numerous customer service awards, and frequent appearances on lists of the best companies to work for.

Selecting or developing leaders for the future requires a forward-looking strategy and culture

The chief executive of an agriculture business was planning to retire, spurring rumors about a hostile takeover. The CEO was actively grooming a successor, an insider who had been with the company for more than 20 years. Our analysis revealed an organizational culture that strongly emphasized *caring* and *purpose*. As one leader reflected, "You feel like part of a large family when you become an employee at this company."

The potential successor understood the culture but was far more risk-averse (*safety*) and respectful of traditions (*order*) than the rest of the company. Given the takeover rumors, top leaders and managers told the CEO that they believed the company needed to take a more aggressive and action-oriented stance in the future. The board decided to consider the internal candidate alongside people from outside the company.

Three external candidates emerged: one who was aligned with the current culture (*purpose*), one who would be a risk-taker and innovative (*learning*), and one who was hard-driving and competitive (*authority*). After considerable deliberation, the board chose the highly competitive leader with the *authority* style. Soon afterward an activist investor attempted a hostile takeover, and the new CEO was able to navigate through the precarious situation, keep the company independent, and simultaneously begin to restructure in preparation for growth.

In a merger, designing a new culture on the basis of complementary strengths can speed up integration and create more value over time

Mergers and acquisitions can either create or destroy value. Numerous studies have shown that cultural dynamics represent one of the greatest yet most frequently overlooked determinants of integration success and postmerger performance.

For example, senior leaders from two merging international food retailers had invested heavily in their organizations' cultures and wanted to preserve their unique strengths and distinct heritages. An assessment of the cultures revealed shared values and areas of compatibility that could provide a foundation for the combined culture, along with important differences for which leaders would have to plan: Both companies emphasized *results, caring,* and *order* and valued high-quality food, good service, treating employees fairly, and maintaining a local mindset. But one operated in a more top-down manner and scored much higher on *authority,* especially in the behavior of leaders.

Because both companies valued teamwork and investments in the local community, the leaders prioritized *caring* and *purpose.* At the same time, their strategy required that they shift from top-down *authority* to a *learning* style that would encourage innovation in new-store formats and online retailing. As one senior leader said of the strategic aspiration, "We need to dare to do things differently, not play by the old rule books."

Once they had agreed on a culture, a rigorous assessment process identified leaders at both organizations whose personal style and values would allow them to serve as bridges to and champions for it. Then a program was launched to promote cultural alignment within 30 top teams, with an emphasis on clarifying priorities, making authentic connections, and developing team norms that would bring the new culture to life.

Finally, structural elements of the new organization were redesigned with culture in mind. A model for leadership was developed that encompassed recruitment, talent assessment, training and development, performance management, reward systems, and promotions. Such design considerations are often overlooked during organizational change, but if systems and structures don't align with cultural and leadership imperatives, progress can be derailed.

In a dynamic, uncertain environment, in which organizations must be more agile, *learning* gains importance

It's not surprising that *results* is the most common culture style among all the companies we have studied. Yet during a decade of helping leaders design aspirational cultures, we have seen a clear trend toward prioritizing *learning* to promote innovation and agility as businesses respond to increasingly less predictable and more complex environments. And although *learning* ranks fourth within our broader database, small companies (200 employees or fewer) and those in newer industries (such as software, technology, and wireless equipment) accord it higher values.

Consider one Silicon Valley–based technology company we worked with. Though it had built a strong business and invested in unique technology and top engineering talent, its revenue growth was starting to decline as newer, nimbler competitors made strides in a field exploding with innovation and business model disruption. Company leaders viewed the culture as a differentiator for the business and decided to diagnose, strengthen, and evolve it. We found a culture that was intensely *results* focused, team based (*caring*), and exploratory (a combination of *enjoyment* and *learning*).

After examining the overall business strategy and gaining input from employees, leaders aimed for a culture that was even more focused on *learning* and adopted our framework as a new language for the organization in its daily work. They initiated conversations between managers and employees about how to emphasize innovation and exploration. Although it takes time to change a culture, we found that the company had made notable progress just one year later. And even as it prepared for an impending sale amid ever greater competition and consolidation, employee engagement scores were on the rise.

A strong culture can be a significant liability when it is misaligned with strategy

We studied a Europe-based industrial services organization whose industry began to experience rapid and unprecedented changes in customer expectations, regulatory demands, and competitive dynamics. The company's strategy, which had historically emphasized cost leadership, needed to shift toward greater service differentiation in response. But its strong culture presented a roadblock to success.

We diagnosed the culture as highly *results* oriented, *caring,* and *order* seeking, with a top-down emphasis on *authority.* The company's leaders decided to shape it to be much more *purpose*-driven, enabling, open, and team based, which would entail an increase in *caring* along with *learning* and *purpose* and a decrease in *authority* and *results.*

This shift was particularly challenging because the current culture had served the organization well for many years, while the industry emphasized efficiency and *results.* Most managers still viewed it as a strength and fought to preserve it, threatening success for the new strategic direction.

Cultural change is daunting for any organization, but as this company realized, it's not impossible. The CEO introduced new leadership development and team coaching programs and training opportunities that would help leaders feel more comfortable with cultural evolution. When people departed, the company carefully selected new leaders who would provide supporting values, such as *caring,* and increased the emphasis on a shared *purpose.* The benefits of this strategic and cultural shift took the form of an increasingly diverse array of integrated service offerings and strong growth, particularly in emerging markets.

Four Levers for Evolving a Culture

Unlike developing and executing a business plan, changing a company's culture is inextricable from the emotional and social dynamics of people in the organization. We have found that four practices in particular lead to successful culture change:

Articulate the aspiration

Much like defining a new strategy, creating a new culture should begin with an analysis of the current one, using a framework that can be openly discussed throughout the organization. Leaders must understand what outcomes the culture produces and how it does or doesn't align with current and anticipated market and business conditions. For example, if the company's primary culture styles are *results* and *authority* but it exists in a rapidly changing industry, shifting toward *learning* or *enjoyment* (while maintaining a focus on *results*) may be appropriate.

An aspirational culture suggests the high-level principles that guide organizational initiatives, as at the technology company that sought to boost agility and flexibility amid increasing competition. Change might be framed in terms of real and present business challenges and opportunities as well as aspirations and trends. Because of culture's somewhat ambiguous and hidden nature, referring to tangible problems, such as market pressures or the challenges of growth, helps people better understand and connect to the need for change.

Select and develop leaders who align with the target culture

Leaders serve as important catalysts for change by encouraging it at all levels and creating a safe climate and what Edgar Schein calls "practice fields." Candidates for recruitment should be evaluated on their alignment with the target. A single model that can assess both organizational culture and individual leadership styles is critical for this activity.

Incumbent leaders who are unsupportive of desired change can be engaged and re-energized through training and education about the important relationship between culture and strategic direction. Often they will support the change after they understand its relevance, its anticipated benefits, and the impact that they personally can have on moving the organization toward the aspiration. However, culture change can and does lead to turnover: Some people move on because they feel they are no longer a good fit for the organization, and others are asked to leave if they jeopardize needed evolution.

Use organizational conversations about culture to underscore the importance of change

To shift the shared norms, beliefs, and implicit understandings within an organization, colleagues can talk one another through the change. Our integrated culture framework can be used to discuss current and desired culture styles and also differences in how senior leaders operate. As employees start to recognize that their leaders are talking about new business outcomes—innovation instead of quarterly earnings, for example—they will begin to behave differently themselves, creating a positive feedback loop.

Various kinds of organizational conversations, such as road shows, listening tours, and structured group discussion, can support change. Social media platforms encourage conversations between senior managers and frontline employees. Influential change champions can advocate for a culture shift through their language and actions. The technology company made a meaningful change in its culture and employee engagement by creating a structured framework for dialogue and cultivating widespread discussion.

Reinforce the desired change through organizational design

When a company's structures, systems, and processes are aligned and support the aspirational culture and strategy, instigating new culture styles and behaviors will become far easier. For example, performance management can be used to encourage employees to embody aspirational cultural attributes. Training practices can reinforce the target culture as the organization grows and adds new people. The degree of centralization and the number of hierarchical levels in the organizational structure can be adjusted to reinforce behaviors inherent to the aspirational culture. Leading scholars such as Henry Mintzberg have shown how organizational structure and other design features can have a profound impact over time on how people think and behave within an organization.

Putting It All Together

All four levers came together at a traditional manufacturer that was trying to become a full solutions provider. The change started with reformulating the strategy and was reinforced by a major brand campaign. But the president understood that the company's culture represented the biggest barrier to change and that the top leaders were the greatest lever for evolving the culture.

The culture was characterized by a drive for *results* followed by *caring* and *purpose,* the last of which was unusually strong for the industry. One employee described the company as "a talented and committed group of people focused on doing good for the planet, with genuine desire, support, and encouragement to make a difference in the community." Whereas the broader culture was highly collaborative, with flat decision-making, leaders were seen as top-down, hierarchical, and sometimes political, which discouraged risk-taking.

The top leaders reviewed their culture's strengths and the gaps in their own styles and discussed what was needed to achieve their strategic aspirations. They agreed that they needed more risk-taking and autonomy and less hierarchy and centralized decision-making. The president restructured the leadership team around strong business line leaders, freeing up time to become a better advocate for the culture and to focus more on customers.

The top team then invited a group of 100 middle managers into the conversation through a series of biannual leadership conferences. The first one established a platform for input, feedback, and the cocreation of an organizational change plan with clear cultural priorities. The president organized these managers into teams focused on critical business challenges. Each team was required to go outside the company to source ideas, to develop solutions, and to present its findings to the group for feedback. This initiative placed middle managers in change roles that would traditionally have been filled by vice presidents, giving them greater autonomy in fostering a *learning*-based culture. The intent was to create real benefits for the business while evolving the culture.

The president also initiated a program to identify employees who had positive disruptive ideas and working styles. These people were put on project teams that addressed key innovation priorities. The teams immediately began improving business results, both in core commercial metrics and in culture and engagement. After only one year employee engagement scores jumped a full 10 points, and customer Net Promoter Scores reached an all-time high—providing strong client references for the company's new and innovative solutions.

It is possible—in fact, vital—to improve organizational performance through culture change, using the simple but powerful models and methods in this article. First leaders must become aware of the culture that operates in their organization. Next they can define an aspirational target culture. Finally they can master the core change practices of articulation of the aspiration, leadership alignment, organizational conversation, and organizational design. Leading with culture may be among the few sources of sustainable competitive advantage left to companies today. Successful leaders will stop regarding culture with frustration and instead use it as a fundamental management tool.

What's Your Organization's Cultural Profile?

BEFORE YOU BEGIN AN INITIATIVE to shape your organization's culture, it's important to explore where it is today. This worksheet and the questions that follow can help you formulate a preliminary assessment of your culture and get the conversation started.

Consider how your organization currently operates, what is valued, how people behave, and what unifies them. Partner with a colleague and independently rate each statement according to how well it describes your organization.

Add the two ratings in each row and then rank the eight styles. The higher the total, the stronger the match.

Compare your rankings with your colleague's and discuss the following questions:

- What do you like most about the current culture?

- What behaviors and mindsets might you evolve?

- How effective are your organization's leaders at role modeling the culture?

- What are the characteristics of people who are most successful in your culture?

- When new people don't succeed in your culture, what is the most common reason?

On a scale of 1–5, rate how well each of these statements describes your organization

1 = Not at all well; 2 = Not very well; 3 = Somewhat well; 4 = Very well; 5 = Extremely well

The organization is focused on:					The organization feels like:					Total
Collaboration and mutual trust					A big family					Caring
1	2	3	4	5	1	2	3	4	5	
Compassion and tolerance					An idealistic community or cause					Purpose
1	2	3	4	5	1	2	3	4	5	
Exploration and creativity					A dynamic project					Learning
1	2	3	4	5	1	2	3	4	5	
Fun and excitement					A celebration					Enjoyment
1	2	3	4	5	1	2	3	4	5	
Achievement and winning					A meritocracy					Results
1	2	3	4	5	1	2	3	4	5	
Strength and boldness					A competitive arena					Authority
1	2	3	4	5	1	2	3	4	5	
Planning and caution					A meticulously planned operation					Safety
1	2	3	4	5	1	2	3	4	5	
Structure and stability					A smoothly running machine					Order
1	2	3	4	5	1	2	3	4	5	

To see an expanded version of the assessment, go to https://hbr.org/2018/01/whats-your-organizations-cultural-profile.

How to Shape Your Culture

FIRST YOU MUST IDENTIFY CULTURE TARGETS. The best ones have some attributes in common: They align with the company's strategic direction; they're important to execute; and they reflect the demands of the external business environment. A good target should be both specific and achievable. For example, "We value our customers" can create ambiguity and lead to inconsistent choices regarding hiring, developing leaders, and running the company. A better version might be "We build genuine and positive relationships with customers; we serve our customers with humility; and we act as ambassadors for our rich brand heritage."

To Set a Culture Target:

Understand the current culture

Examine your culture—the company's founding and heritage, its espoused values, subcultures, leadership style, and team dynamics. (Use the preceding assessment to start the conversation.)

Identify your culture's strengths and examine its impact on your organization today. Interview key stakeholders and influential members of the organization as needed.

Consider strategy and the environment

Assess current and future external conditions and strategic choices and determine which cultural styles will need to be strengthened or diminished in response.

Formulate a culture target according to which styles will support future changes.

Frame the aspiration in business realities

Translate the target into organizational change priorities. It should be framed not as a culture change initiative but in terms of real-world problems to be solved and solutions that create value.

Focus on *leadership alignment, organizational conversations,* and *organizational design* as the levers to guide the culture's evolution.

One Company's Experience

One large company used its search for a new director as an opportunity to bridge a problematic gap between the company's culture and the board's culture. To accomplish this, the leadership first diagnosed the two cultures along with its aspirations for the new director.

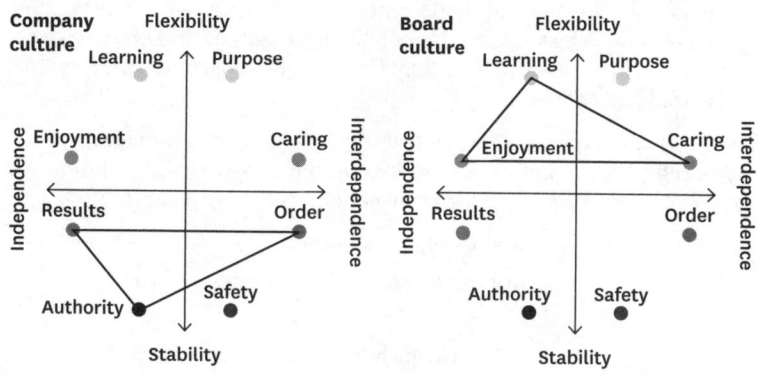

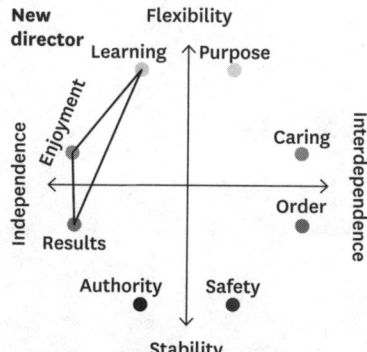

Whereas the company was highly *results* oriented and focused on *order*, discipline, and execution, the board was far more *learning* oriented, exploratory, inquisitive, and focused on *enjoyment*. A director who was *results* driven and curious would help bridge the two cultures.

Two years after an individual with the desired style was brought in, the board and the management team reported more-effective strategic planning activities and improved company performance.

Convergence Matters

WHEN WE COMPARED EMPLOYEES' VIEWS on their organization's most salient cultural attributes, two types of organizations emerged: *low convergence* (employees rarely agreed on the most important cultural attributes) and *high convergence* (views were more closely aligned). In the two examples below, each dot represents one employee.

Note that in the low-convergence organization, seven of the eight cultural attributes were cited as most important, and every quadrant is represented. That means employees viewed their company in varying and often opposite ways. Some saw a *caring* organization, for example, while others saw one that emphasized *authority*.

Why is high convergence important? Because it correlates with levels of employee engagement and customer orientation. However, if the culture you have is not the one you want, high convergence will make it harder to change.

Company A: Low convergence

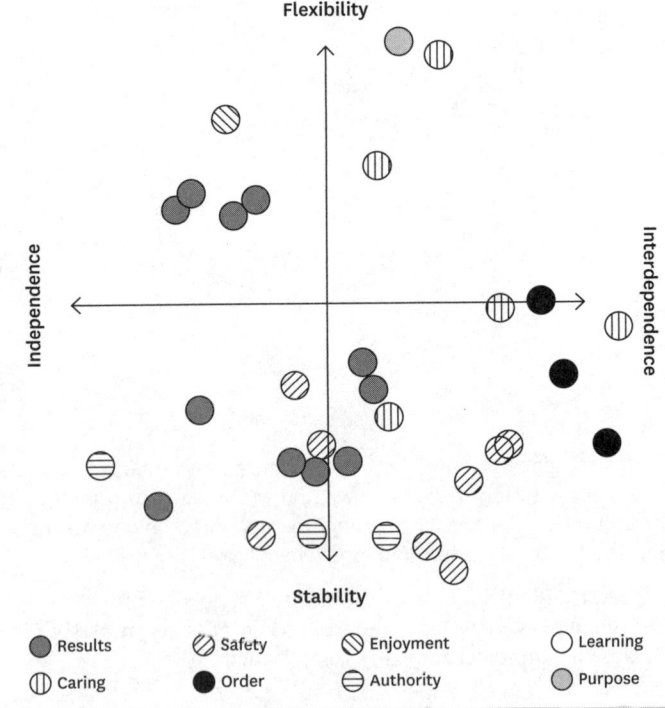

Company B: High convergence

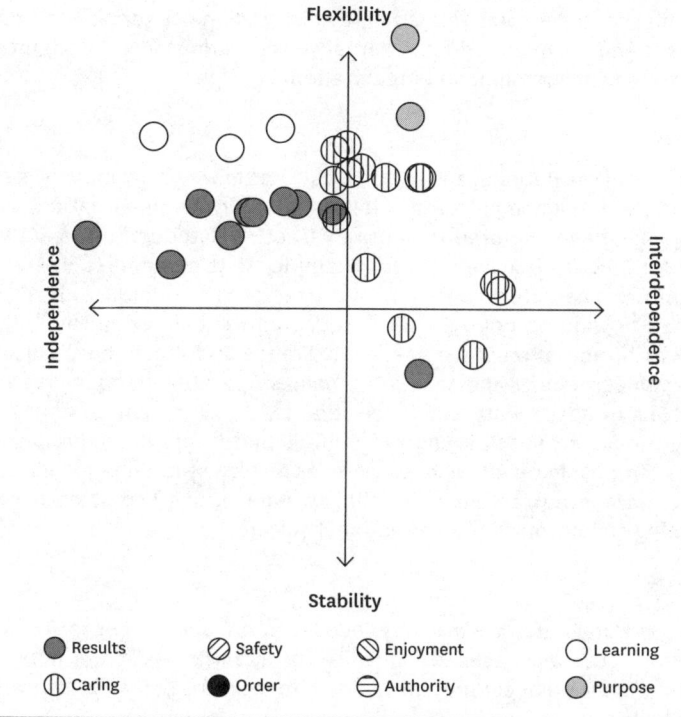

Context, Conditions, and Culture

CONTEXT MATTERS WHEN ASSESSING a culture's strategic effectiveness.

Leaders must simultaneously consider culture styles and key organizational and market conditions if they want their culture to help drive performance. Region and industry are among the most germane external factors to keep in mind; critical internal considerations include alignment with strategy, leadership, and organizational design.

Region

The values of the national and regional cultures in which a company is embedded can influence patterns of behavior within the organization. (This linkage has been explored in depth by Geert Hofstede and the authors of the GLOBE study.) We find, for example, that companies operating in countries characterized by a high degree of institutional collectivism (defined as valuing equity within groups and encouraging the collective distribution of resources), such as France and Brazil, have cultures that emphasize *order* and *safety*. Companies operating in countries with low levels of uncertainty avoidance (that is, they are open to ambiguity and future uncertainty), such as the United States and Australia, place a greater emphasis on *learning, purpose,* and *enjoyment.* Such external influences are important considerations when working across borders or designing an appropriate organizational culture.

Industry

Varying cultural attributes may be needed to address industry-specific regulations and customer needs. A comparison of organizations across industries reveals evidence that cultures might adapt to meet the demands of industry environments.

Organizational cultures in financial services are more likely to emphasize *safety.* Given the increasingly complex regulations enacted in response to the financial crisis, careful work and risk management are more critical than ever in this industry. In contrast, nonprofits are far more *purpose*-driven, which can reinforce their commitment to a mission by aligning employee behavior around a common goal.

Culture styles ranked by industry

Based on an assessment of 230+ companies (industry) and a subsample of 25 companies (strategy)

Strategy

For its full benefit to be realized, a culture must support the strategic goals and plans of the business. For example, we find differences between companies that adopt a differentiation strategy and companies that pursue a cost leadership strategy. Although *results* and *caring* are key cultural characteristics at both types of companies, *enjoyment, learning,* and *purpose* are more suited to differentiation, whereas *order* and *authority* are more suited to cost leadership. Flexible cultures—which emphasize *enjoyment* and *learning*—can spur product innovation in companies aiming to differentiate themselves, whereas stable and predictable cultures, which emphasize *order* and *authority*, can help maintain operational efficiency to keep costs low.

Strategic considerations related to a company's life cycle are also linked to organizational culture. Companies with a strategy that seeks to stabilize or maintain their market position prioritize *learning*, whereas organizations operating with a turnaround strategy tend to prioritize *order* and *safety* in their efforts to redirect or reorganize unprofitable units.

Culture styles ranked by strategy

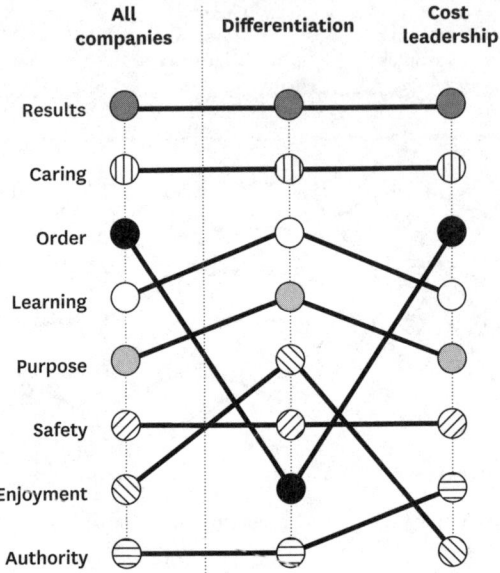

Based on an assessment of 230+ companies (industry) and a subsample of 25 companies (strategy)

Leadership

It is hard to overestimate the importance of aligning culture and leadership. The character and behaviors of a CEO and top executives can have a profound effect on culture. Conversely, culture serves to either constrain or enhance the performance of leaders. Our own data from executive recruiting activities shows that a lack of cultural fit is responsible for up to 68% of new-hire failures at the senior leadership level. For individual leaders, cultural fit is as important as capabilities and experience.

Organizational design

We see a two-way relationship between a company's culture and its particular structure. In many cases, structure and systems follow culture. For example, companies that prioritize teamwork and collaboration might design incentive systems that include shared team and company goals along with rewards that recognize collective effort. However, a long-standing organizational design choice can lead to the formation of a culture. Because the latter is far more difficult to alter, we suggest that structural changes should be aligned with the desired culture.

About the Research

WE UNDERTOOK A COMPREHENSIVE STUDY of organizational culture and outcomes to explore the link between them. We analyzed the cultures of more than 230 companies along with the leadership styles and values of more than 1,300 executives across a range of industries (including consumer discretionary, consumer staples, energy and utilities, financial and professional services, health care, industrials, and IT and telecommunications), regions (Africa, Asia, Europe, the Middle East, North America, Oceania, and South America), and organizational types (public, private, and nonprofit). We diagnosed those cultures using online survey responses from approximately 25,000 employees together with interviews of company managers.

Our analysis highlighted how strongly each of the eight styles defined the organizations in our study. *Results* ranked first, and *caring* second. This pattern is consistent across company types, company sizes, regions, and industries. *Order* and *learning* ranked among the third and fourth most common styles in many cultures.

Culture appears to most directly affect employee engagement and motivation, followed by customer orientation. To model its relationship to organizational outcomes, we assessed employee engagement levels for all the companies using widely accepted survey questions and arrived at customer-orientation scores with an online questionnaire. In many cases we also documented top leaders' individual styles and values.

We found that employee engagement is most strongly related to greater flexibility, in the form of *enjoyment, learning, purpose,* and *caring*. Similarly, we observed a positive relationship between customer orientation and those four styles plus *results*. These relationships, too, are surprisingly consistent across companies. We also found that engagement and customer orientation are stronger when employees are in close agreement about the culture's characteristics.

Our research was influenced by the work of countless scholars in this field, many of whom are mentioned in this article. In addition, we stand on the shoulders of giants such as David Caldwell, Jennifer Chatman, James Heskett, John Kotter, Charles O'Reilly, and many, many others who have inspired our thinking.

Originally published in January–February 2018. Reprint R1801B

Getting Serious About Diversity

by Robin J. Ely and David A. Thomas

"THE BUSINESS CASE HAS BEEN MADE to demonstrate the value a diverse board brings to the company and its constituents."

"The case for establishing a truly diverse workforce, at all organizational levels, grows more compelling each year. . . . The financial impact—as proven by multiple studies—makes this a no-brainer."

"The business case is clear: When women are at the table, the discussion is richer, the decision-making process is better, and the organization is stronger."

These rallying cries for more diversity in companies, from recent statements by CEOs, are representative of what we hear from business leaders around the world. They have three things in common: All articulate a business case for hiring more women or people of color; all demonstrate good intentions; and none of the claims is actually supported by robust research findings.

We say this as scholars who were among the first to demonstrate the potential benefits of more race and gender heterogeneity in organizations. In 1996 we published an HBR article, "Making Differences Matter: A New Paradigm for Managing Diversity," in which we argued that companies adopting a radically new way of understanding and leveraging diversity could reap the real and full benefits of a diverse workforce. This new way entailed not only recruiting and retaining more people from underrepresented "identity groups" but also tapping their identity-related knowledge and experiences as resources for learning how the organization could perform its core work better. Our research showed that when companies take this approach, their teams are more effective than either homogeneous teams or diverse teams that don't learn from their members' differences. Such companies send a message that varied points of view are valued and don't need to be suppressed for the sake of group cohesion. This attitude encourages employees to rethink how work gets done and how best to achieve their goals.

We called this approach the *learning-and-effectiveness paradigm*. We argued that cultivating a learning orientation toward diversity—one in which people draw on their experiences as members of particular identity groups to reconceive tasks, products, business processes, and organizational norms—enables companies to increase their effectiveness. We stand by the research on which that article was based, and we continue to advocate its conclusions.

The problem is that nearly 25 years later, organizations have largely failed to adopt a learning orientation toward diversity and are no closer to reaping its benefits. Instead, business leaders and diversity advocates alike are advancing a simplistic and empirically unsubstantiated version of the business case. They misconstrue or ignore what abundant research has now made clear: Increasing the numbers of traditionally underrepresented people in your workforce does not *automatically* produce benefits. Taking an "add diversity and stir" approach, while business continues as usual, will not spur leaps in your firm's effectiveness or financial performance.

And despite all the rhetoric about the value of diversity, white women and people of color remain seriously underrepresented in many industries and in most companies' senior ranks. That lack of progress suggests that top executives don't actually find the business case terribly compelling.

On that point, we have to agree: The *simplistic* business case isn't persuasive. A credible and powerful case *can* be made, however, with three critical modifications. First, platitudes must give way to sound, empirically based conclusions. Second, business leaders must reject the notion that maximizing shareholder returns is paramount; instead they must embrace a broader vision of success

Idea in Brief

The Context

Business leaders often make a business case for diversity, claiming that hiring more women or people of color results in better financial performance.

The Problem

There's no empirical evidence that simply diversifying the workforce, absent fundamental changes to the organizational culture, makes a company more profitable.

A Better Approach

Companies *can* benefit from diversity if leaders create a psychologically safe workplace, combat systems of discrimination and subordination, embrace the styles of employees from different identity groups, and make cultural differences a resource for learning and improving organizational effectiveness.

that encompasses learning, innovation, creativity, flexibility, equity, and human dignity. Finally, leaders must acknowledge that increasing demographic diversity does not, by itself, increase effectiveness; what matters is how an organization harnesses diversity, and whether it's willing to reshape its power structure.

In this article we expose the flaws in the current diversity rhetoric and then outline what a 21st-century learning-and-effectiveness paradigm could look like—and how leaders can foster it.

A Critique of the Business Case for Diversity

Let's start with the claim that putting more women on corporate boards leads to economic gains. That's a fallacy, probably fueled by studies that went viral a decade ago reporting that the more women directors a company has, the better its financial performance. But those studies show correlations, not causality. In all likelihood, some other factor—such as industry or firm size—is responsible for both increases in the number of women directors and improvement in a firm's performance.

In any case, the research touting the link was conducted by consulting firms and financial institutions and fails to pass muster when subjected to scholarly scrutiny. Meta-analyses of rigorous, peer-reviewed studies found no significant relationships—causal or otherwise—between board gender diversity and firm performance. That could be because women directors may not differ from their male counterparts in the characteristics presumed to affect board decisions, and even if they do differ, their voices may be marginalized. What is more pertinent, however, is that board decisions are typically too far removed from firms' bottom-line performance to exert a direct or unconditional effect.

As for studies citing the positive impact of racial diversity on corporate financial performance, they do not stand up to scrutiny either. Indeed, we know of no evidence to suggest that replacing, say, two or three white male directors with people from underrepresented groups is likely to enhance the profits of a *Fortune* 500 company.

The economic argument for diversity is no more valid when it's applied to changing the makeup of the overall workforce. A 2015 survey of Harvard Business School alumni revealed that 76% of those in senior executive positions believe that "a more diverse workforce improves the organization's financial performance." But scholarly researchers have rarely found that increased diversity leads to improved financial outcomes. They *have* found that it leads to higher-quality work, better decision-making, greater team satisfaction, and more equality—under certain circumstances. Although those outcomes could conceivably make some aspects of the business more profitable, they would need to be extraordinarily consequential to affect a firm's bottom line.

Moreover, advocates who justify diversity initiatives on the basis of financial benefits may be shooting themselves in the foot. Research suggests that when company diversity statements emphasize the economic payoffs, people from underrepresented groups start questioning whether the organization is a place where they really belong, which reduces their interest in joining it. In addition, when diversity initiatives promise financial gains but fail to deliver, people are likely to withdraw their support for them.

Still another flaw in the familiar business case for diversity is the notion that a diverse team will have richer discussions and a better decision-making process simply because it is diverse. Having people from various identity groups "at the table" is no guarantee that anything will get better; in fact, research shows that things often get worse, because increasing diversity can increase tensions and conflict. Under the right organizational conditions, though, employees can turn cultural differences into assets for achieving team goals.

Studies have shown, for example, that diverse teams realize performance benefits in certain circumstances: when team members are able to reflect on and discuss team functioning; when status differences among ethnic groups are minimized; when people from both high- and low-status identity groups believe the team supports learning; and—as we reported in our earlier article—when teams orient members to learn from their differences rather than marginalize or deny them. But absent conditions that foster inquiry, egalitarianism, and learning, diversity either is unrelated to or undermines team effectiveness.

Many progressive companies today recognize the conditional nature of the diversity-performance link and have moved beyond "diversity," the catchword of the 1990s, to "diversity and inclusion." They understand that just increasing the number of people from underrepresented groups is not meaningful if those employees do not feel valued and respected. We applaud the emphasis on inclusion, but it is insufficient because it doesn't fundamentally reconfigure power relations.

Being genuinely valued and respected involves more than just feeling included. It involves having the power to help set the agenda, influence what—and how—work is done, have one's needs and interests taken into account, and have one's contributions recognized and rewarded with further opportunities to contribute and advance. Undertaking this shift in power is what the learning-and-effectiveness companies we wrote about in 1996 were doing, and it's what enabled them to tap diversity's true benefits.

The Learning-and-Effectiveness Paradigm, Redux

What we've learned since we wrote our original article is that embracing a learning orientation toward diversity turns out to be quite difficult. To make real progress, people—and the organizational cultures they inhabit—must change. But instead of doing the hard work involved, companies have generally stuck with easier, more limited approaches that don't alter the status quo.

We previously identified four actions that were helping business leaders and managers shift to a learning-and-effectiveness approach. We still consider those actions fundamental, but we present them anew here to underscore the message in light of today's challenges and opportunities.

Build trust

The first task for those in charge is to build trust by creating a workplace where people feel safe expressing themselves freely. That requires setting a tone of honest discourse and getting comfortable with vulnerability—one's own and others'.

At no time has this need been greater in the United States than during the current unrest spurred by outrage over police brutality against Black men and women—a legacy of centuries of racism. Two weeks into the nationwide protests that began in May, white leaders in companies across the country struggled with how to respond. Publicly expressing support for the Black Lives Matter movement was one thing; knowing what to say to Black employees, who might already have been feeling marginalized or undervalued at work, was quite another. Leaders who were used to wielding authority grounded in their subject-matter expertise had no comparable expertise to handle the deep grief, rage, and despair felt by many of their employees—especially their Black employees. And Black leaders, many with first-hand experience of police mistreatment and other forms of racial oppression, faced the challenge of managing their own strong emotions and speaking their truth without appearing biased against whites.

Yet troubling times provide opportunities for leaders to begin conversations that foster learning. In response to public acts of racial injustice, for example, white leaders can reach out from a place of vulnerability, as a way of creating connection and psychological safety, rather than staying silent from a place of privilege and self-protection. This was the choice made by a white senior partner in a global professional services firm when he decided to convene a special virtual meeting with his teams across the country. He knew that if he said nothing about the recent racist incidents, his silence would speak for him, with a message not of neutrality but of complicity. Just weeks before, he'd been eloquent in addressing the distress wrought by the Covid-19 pandemic, but when it came to race, he felt at a complete loss. What he astutely realized, though, was that people needed him simply to begin a dialogue, acknowledge his pain and theirs, and give them the space to talk about their experiences inside and outside the firm, if they wished. He had no solutions, but that moment required none—just a willingness to speak from the heart and listen compassionately to whatever his colleagues might share. Perhaps most important, he was willing to risk not getting his own words or actions exactly right, and he was ready to receive feedback with openness and equanimity.

Actively work against discrimination and subordination

Creating psychological safety and building employees' trust can be an excellent starting point for the second action: taking concrete measures to combat forms of discrimination and subordination that inhibit employees' ability to thrive. This action calls for both individual and collective learning aimed at producing systemic change.

Over the years we've seen the emergence of a multibillion-dollar industry dedicated to advancing such goals. Companies have adopted a slew of initiatives as a result: affinity groups, mentoring programs, work-family accommodation policies, and unconscious-bias training, to name a few. But the sad truth is that these efforts largely fail to produce meaningful, sustained change—and sometimes even backfire.

Leaders are the stewards of an organization's culture; their behaviors and mindsets reverberate throughout the organization. Hence to dismantle systems of discrimination and subordination, leaders must undergo the same shifts of heart, mind, and behavior that they want for the organization as a whole and then translate those personal shifts into real, lasting change in their companies.

To that end, a first step for leaders is to learn about how systems of privilege and oppression—racism, sexism, ethnocentrism, classism, heterosexism—operate in the wider culture. Numerous excellent books and articles can help with this work; they have the added benefit of relieving those on the receiving end of oppressive systems from the burden of educating their majority-group counterparts. And the impact can be surprising. For example, major news organizations picked up the story of a Black flight attendant who noticed a white male passenger reading a book about white people's reluctance to confront racism. She struck up a conversation with the man and had a moving exchange with him, eventually learning that he was the CEO of a major airline. The encounter filled her with hope: Here was a powerful executive—someone in a position to effect change—making a genuine effort to understand systemic racism.

Educating oneself is important, but it will be meaningless unless leaders take the next step: investigating how their organization's culture has reproduced systems of oppression, undercutting some groups' opportunities to thrive and succeed, while giving others a boost. As part of that investigation, leaders must examine what stereotypes and assumptions they hold about employees' competencies and suitability for jobs, acknowledge that they have blind spots, and come to see how their personal defenses can shut down learning—their own and their organization's. Working with hundreds of leaders over the years, we have seen how this individual learning journey can be a transformational experience that often leads to individual behavioral change.

But that's not enough. The critical final step in rooting out systems of discrimination and subordination is for leaders to use their personal experience to spur collective learning and systemic change. It is here that even the most progressive leaders' efforts tend to stall. Such efforts require a well-articulated, widely shared organizational mission to motivate and guide change, together with a collective process of continuous reflection and consciousness-raising, experimentation, and action—followed by sustained attention, monitoring each change for impact, and making adjustments accordingly.

An example of this process comes from a midsize consulting firm whose partners—almost all white men—had begun to fear that high turnover among the white women and people of color they employed meant they were losing talent, potentially undermining the firm's competitiveness. Taking a hard look at their culture, they identified a flawed approach to project assignment that was inadvertently contributing to systematic inequities. Plum projects were going disproportionately to white men; it was the old story of people having an easier time identifying talent when it comes in a package that looks like them. When a particularly challenging project for an important client came up—the kind that can stretch and give exposure to a promising young consultant—the white male partners staffed it with their go-to people: other white men. Meanwhile, white women and people of color, despite having been recruited from the same highly competitive MBA programs as their white male counterparts, regularly were assigned the more mundane projects. They got stuck doing tasks they had long ago mastered, which led many to leave the firm. Come promotion time, the few who remained were either counseled out or told they still weren't ready for partnership; women waited two years longer than men, on average, to make partner.

But were the go-to people actually better? Did they really have more "raw horsepower," as the partners believed? When those leaders examined their developmental practices, they were chagrined to see clear patterns in who received coaching, whose mistakes were forgiven, and who got second and even third chances to prove themselves: the white men. So after an uncomfortable reckoning with their biases, the partners decided to experiment with making comparable investments in people they'd previously overlooked—people they might have automatically, if not quite consciously, written off simply as hires to meet diversity goals. When they started treating white women and people of color more like the white men they'd favored, they were surprised to find a bigger, more diverse pool of talent than they'd expected.

Embrace a wide range of styles and voices

The third necessary action for leaders and managers involves actively trying to understand how organizational norms might implicitly discourage certain behavioral styles or silence certain voices. For example, in companies where the prototypical leader is a white man who earns respect by speaking assertively, women and Black men, who are often penalized for being assertive, may find themselves in a double bind: They can conform to the organization's norms and deviate from cultural prescriptions for their group, or they can do the opposite. But either way, they violate one set of expectations, risking marginalization and diminished chances for advancement.

Managers may believe they're giving helpful feedback when they tell a large Black man to smile more so that his white colleagues won't fear him, when they ask a Latina who advocates passionately for a project to dial it down, when they encourage a no-nonsense white woman to be "nicer," or when they urge a soft-spoken woman of East Asian descent to speak more forcefully. But all such messages communicate that these employees must be ever-mindful of how others see them in relation to stereotyped images of their group, making it harder for them to bring their talents and perspectives to the table. Companies need performance management systems that tie feedback and evaluation criteria to bona fide task requirements rather than group stereotypes.

Make cultural differences a resource for learning

For companies shifting to a learning-and-effectiveness paradigm, the fourth action is to encourage—and draw lessons from—open discussions about how identity groups shape employees' experiences inside and outside the organization. Leaders should frame those experiences as a valid source of ideas for enhancing the organization's work and culture. Even if employees champion ideas that are at odds with the company's profit goals, those ideas may still be worth pursuing if they help the organization achieve its mission or uphold its values.

Over the years, we have seen that learning from cultural differences is more likely to occur once the previous three actions are under way: Leaders have created trust, begun to dismantle systems of discrimination and subordination, and embraced a broad range of styles. Without such efforts, talking about differences happens (if it happens at all) only in reaction to diversity-related crises—when discussions tend to be fraught and people's capacity to learn is diminished.

An example of learning from gender diversity comes from Boris Groysberg's study of top-ranked research analysts on Wall Street. In exploring whether they take their star status with them when they switch firms, he found a fascinating sex difference: Unlike their male counterparts, whose performance worsened upon changing firms, women who made a move experienced no such performance drop. The reason, Groysberg concluded, was that women analysts faced sex discrimination, and so they had to do the job differently from men. Women had a more difficult time building support networks inside their firm, had fewer mentors, and were neglected by high-status groups such as the firm's institutional sales force—an important source of industry information. And so, unlike men, women built their franchises on portable, external relationships with clients, companies, and the media. In addition, they forged unconventional in-house relationships with their firm's retail sales force—also an important source of industry information but a low-status group that male analysts typically ignored. Not only were women stars able to maintain their performance upon switching firms but, generally speaking, they outperformed their male peers over the nine-year period of the study. In short, women were not only different; they were better.

In a follow-up set of case studies, coauthored with Ashish Nanda and Laura Morgan Roberts, respectively, Groysberg showed how a Wall Street firm's research director leveraged women's "difference" to everyone's advantage. He aggressively recruited talented women for the analyst role and then set out to create the conditions that would enable them to thrive, emphasizing team culture, allowing flexible work arrangements, and instituting systems that gave analysts regular, unbiased feedback to help them set personal improvement goals. Additionally, he encouraged people to develop their own style and voice. As one woman star in the firm noted, "We have always been given the freedom to be ourselves." Another said, "I never felt I had to pretend to be male to fit in here." Within three years this firm had the highest percentage of top-ranked women analysts of any firm on Wall Street and the lowest rate of female turnover. Furthermore, the research department moved in the rankings from 15th to first, and the unique approach that women had developed for building their franchises became the basis for training all the firm's analysts. What the research director figured out was that gender had given women analysts a unique set of experiences, and those, together with their resilience and ingenuity, led to new insights into how to do the job better.

We have also seen how the mere act of learning across employees' differences can have a positive impact, even when the content of the learning is unrelated to people's identities. The benefits are particularly strong when the differences have been historically fraught with tension. In a study of more than 400 retail bank branches in the northeastern United States, we, together with Irene Padavic of Florida State University, found that the more racially diverse the branch, the better its performance—but only for branches in which *all* employees, across all racial groups, experienced the environment as conducive to learning. Some of that learning definitely came from sharing cultural knowledge—for example, a white branch manager described how his Chinese coworker's explanations of norms in the Chinese community helped him better serve that segment of customers. But many of the branches' tasks were technical and unrelated to people's cultural backgrounds. In those cases, the benefit from diversity seemed to stem mainly from the process of learning—a process that involves taking risks and being unafraid to say "I don't know," "I made a mistake," or "I need help." Showing such vulnerability across divisive lines of difference, such as race, and being met with acceptance rather than judgment or rejection, strengthens relationships. Stronger relationships in turn increase resilience in the face of conflict and other stressors. In short, for culturally diverse teams, the experience of learning across racial differences can, in and of itself, improve performance.

Inequality is bad for both business and society. Organizations limit their capacity for innovation and continuous improvement unless all employees are full participants in the enterprise: fully seen, heard, developed, engaged—and rewarded accordingly. Moreover, such treatment can unleash enormous reserves of leadership potential too long suppressed by systems that perpetuate inequality.

When the only legitimate conversation about diversity is one that links it to economic gains, we tend to discount the problem of inequality. In fact, studies have shown that making the economic case diminishes people's sense that equality is itself important, limits socially conscious investors' ability to promote it, and may even increase bias. Furthermore, focusing on financial benefits sends a message to traditionally underrepresented employees that they are worth hiring and investing in only because having "their kind" in the mix increases the firm's profitability.

Companies will not reap benefits from diversity unless they build a culture that insists on equality. Treating differences as a source of knowledge and connection lays the groundwork for such a culture. But as part of that process, firms may have to make financial investments that they won't recoup, at least in the short run, and more will be required of top leaders, managers, and rank-and-file employees alike. Everyone will have to learn how to actively listen to others' perspectives, have difficult conversations, refrain from blame and judgment, and solicit feedback about how their behaviors and company practices might be impeding the push for a culture that supports learning, equality, and mutual respect. Developing those capacities is no small feat in any context; it is even more challenging for people working across cultural identity differences. But teams that truly embrace the learning-and-effectiveness paradigm will come to understand that homogeneity isn't better; it's just easier. They'll realize, too, that the benefits of diversity arise as much from the collective work of developing those key capacities as from the collective learning they enable.

Finally, while there *is* a business case for diversity—one that rests on sound evidence, an expansive definition of what makes a business successful, and the presence of facilitating conditions—we are disturbed by the implication that there must be economic grounds to justify investing in people from underrepresented groups. Why should anyone need an economic rationale for affirming the agency and dignity of any group of human beings? We should make the necessary investment because doing so honors our own and others' humanity and gives our lives meaning. If company profits come at the price of our humanity, they are costing us too much. And if diversity initiatives fail to reckon with that trade-off, they will amount to little more than rearranging the deck chairs on a sinking ship.

Originally published in November–December 2020. Reprint R2006J

Designing Work
That People Love

by Marcus Buckingham

AS RECORD NUMBERS OF PEOPLE HAVE QUIT their jobs, all sectors of the economy are struggling to fill vacancies. To get people back to work, organizations are changing long-standing policies and offering unprecedented incentives. Transportation companies, for example, have upped their wages to lure long-haul drivers back into truck cabs. California public schools are allowing retired teachers to return to work without recertification. CEOs and CHROs are falling all over themselves to offer flex-time work arrangements more attractive than those of their competitors. But such attempts miss the fundamental problem.

Simply put, work isn't working for us. It wasn't before the pandemic, and it isn't now. According to surveys my colleagues and I have conducted at ADP Research Institute (ADPRI), before the pandemic only 18% of respondents were fully engaged at work, 17% felt highly resilient at work, and 14% trusted their senior leaders and team leader. The Centers for Disease Control and Prevention reported in 2018 that 71% of adults had at least one symptom of workplace stress, such as headaches or feeling overwhelmed or anxious.

The pandemic has added even more pressure to our existing pain. Engagement and resilience are at all-time lows, having each dropped two percentage points during the course of the pandemic. (That may sound like a small change, but given how low those figures already were and the size of the samples, it is both statistically and practically significant.) Meanwhile, a quarter of U.S. workers quit their jobs in 2021—a historic high.

This points to a problem that increasing wages or simplifying professional on-ramps alone won't solve, although those efforts certainly help improve employees' quality of life. We know this because in ADPRI's most recent 50,000-person surveys of stratified random samples of working populations around the world, the most powerful predictors of retention, performance, engagement, resilience, and inclusion did not include pay or liking one's colleagues or work location or even a strong belief in the mission of the organization. All those provided some explanatory power, but none was as significant as these three items:

- Was I excited to work every day last week?

- Did I have a chance to use my strengths every day?

- At work do I get a chance to do what I'm good at and something I love?

These results, neuroscience research, and my decades of experience working with individuals in organizations strongly suggest that only when a company intelligently links what people love to their actual activities will it achieve higher performance, higher engagement and resilience, and lower turnover.

To stem the tide and to attract and retain the best people, then, we must redesign jobs around a simple but powerful concept: love for the content of the work itself. That word may seem strong in this context, but people's affinity for their work can and should reach this level, and when it does, amazing things can happen.

Creating a place where all people can find love in their work means incorporating three principles in everything your business does: *The people are the point.* Employees, rather than customers or shareholders, are the most important stakeholders in your organization. *One size fits one.* Each of those employees is a unique person with distinct loves, interests, and skills. *In trust we grow.* For employees to discover and contribute their loves at work, leaders must explicitly make trust the foundation of all practices and policies.

Idea in Brief

The Problem

Resignations are at an all-time high, and companies desperate to fill vacancies are trying everything from pay raises to trendy perks. But these interventions are falling short—because the real problem is that jobs are often stressful, meaningless, and unlovable.

The Solution

Companies need to take advantage of each person's unique skills and passions. That means making employees the key stakeholders in the organization, minimizing standardization in performance management tools, and trusting people to accomplish their goals in the way they see fit.

The Benefit

Employees don't need to love everything about their jobs, but research shows that a little goes a long way toward reducing burnout and helping with engagement. Companies that have begun to embrace some of the tenets in this article have seen improvements in both retention and overall performance.

We'll take a look at how the most forward-thinking companies are beginning to implement each of these in turn. But first let's examine why love is so important in the workplace and what companies have missed by ignoring it.

What's Love Got to Do with It?

When you're in love with another person, your brain chemistry changes. We don't yet know the exact biochemical cause of romantic love—it appears to be some combination of oxytocin, dopamine, norepinephrine, and vasopressin. But research does reveal that when you're engaged in an activity you love, that same chemical cocktail is present in your brain—along with anandamide, which brings you feelings of joy and wonder.

Primed by this cocktail, you interact with the world differently. Research by neurobiologists suggests that these "love chemicals" lessen the regulatory function of your neocortex, widening your perspective on yourself and liberating your mind to accept new thoughts and feelings. You register other people's emotions more intensely. You remember details more vividly. You perform cognitive tasks faster and better. You are more optimistic, more loyal, more forgiving, and more open to new information and experiences. One could say that doing what you love makes you more effective, but it's so much more than that: You're on fire without the burnout.

So if you're doing work you love, work need not be a stressor but can instead be a source of energy and resilience. Indeed, ADPRI data on engagement shows that people who find love, strength, joy, and excitement in what they do each day are far more likely to be productive, to stay at the company longer than others do, and to sustain themselves in the face of life's inevitable challenges. Finding love in work, therefore, is not self-indulgent or narcissistic; it is a precursor and an amplifier of performance.

To be clear, that's not quite the same as saying that work must consist exclusively of what you love. We have no data proving that the most productive and engaged people at work love *all* they do. What it points to, though, is that if leaders want their employees to be high performing, to stay with the organization, and to be engaged and resilient, they should be intentional in helping them find love in some of what they do, every day.

Data from the Mayo Clinic reinforces this finding and suggests that 20% is a useful threshold. Its research into burnout in doctors and nurses suggests that if less than 20% of your work consists of things you love to do, you are far more likely to experience physical and psychological burnout. Intriguingly, loving *more* than 20% doesn't seem to net much increase in resilience. A little love of what you do at work goes a long, long way.

For many of us, finding even that level of love in our work is challenging. Perhaps daunted by the sheer range of where employees can find love, or perhaps distrustful of their intentions, or perhaps presuming that "no one could love this job," many managers have designed loveless work, in which the job is defined by standardized steps or required competencies, and success is measured by how closely the employee conforms to them. Distribution-center work and delivery-driver roles usually fall into this category.

It's neither fair nor realistic to put the onus on employees who are faced with jobs like those—and with the need to put food on the table—to find the love in what they do, although it's clear from my decades of research into all manner of jobs that people can find love in surprising places. I've interviewed a manufacturing worker who loved to figure out the "personality" of each of the machines he operated and intervene right before one of them "chose" to break down. I've done focus groups with boron miners who revealed passions as diverse as a love of precision, the thrill of figuring out how to go a hundred days without even the most minor safety incident, and simply being part of a team. Slaughterhouse work, long-haul trucking, housekeeping—all these jobs include a range of activities specific enough to serve as the raw material for some love of the work. The fact that we haven't designed those jobs through the lens of people with specific preferences and passions doesn't mean there's no love to be found there.

So let's turn to organizations. It's time to start designing jobs with love in mind. If leaders were to take all this data to heart and deliberately try to create what I call a Love + Work organization, in which a greater percentage of employees find love in what they do— even if only 20% of the time—how would they proceed? They would make sure that engaged and resilient people were uplifted rather than depleted by their jobs, and as a result delivered better services and products to their customers and made more-sustainable commitments to their communities. Although I know of no one organization today that fully embodies the Love + Work ideal, plenty are beginning to implement pieces of the three core principles.

The People Are the Point

A true Love + Work organization is built on a recognition of and commitment to the fundamental importance of each person who comes to work. This stance represents an advance on both Milton Friedman's shareholder capitalism, which held that an organization's sole purpose is to maximize shareholder value, *and* Joseph Stiglitz's stakeholder capitalism, which introduced the idea that organizations should also maximize value to customers, employees, and the broader community.

A Love + Work organization sees employees as the *integrating point* for all other stakeholders rather than as merely one of many. They are, after all, where the work actually happens—where the value in products or for customers is created. That requires that every employee be seen as a full human being, not just a cog in the machine. Specifically, Love + Work organizations do the following:

Recruit human beings, not workers

In a more human-centric approach to onboarding, these companies are rigorous and detailed in explaining why each candidate was selected and what specific strengths and loves they saw in the person, including but also going beyond how those can add value to the overall mission of the organization.

Lululemon is a leader in this. During the company's onboarding process, new employees are encouraged to set goals, both career *and* personal. Employees are equally celebrated whether their goal is to become the company's CEO or to start their own fashion brand sometime in the future. This focus on the person's unique ambitions during onboarding helps lululemon's 90-day retention and first-year employee-engagement levels rise twice as high as industry averages.

Commit to lifelong learning

A Love + Work organization invests in the ongoing education of each employee. That might be in the form of direct payment for college degrees, as at Amazon, Walmart, and others; or forgiving and reimbursing student loans, as Geico, Starbucks, and UPS do; or giving employees a certain amount of discretionary time to pursue their own projects, as Google has periodically done over the years. All these efforts communicate explicitly that the employee's growth and development have intrinsic worth, even if it doesn't immediately accrue to the organization.

Support alumni

A Love + Work organization has a formal and carefully considered offboarding program that reinforces the message that people's worth as human beings extends far beyond their time with the organization. Many companies, including Accenture and McKinsey, have found that staying close to a strong alumni community offers practical benefits in the form of existing client growth and referrals. But it's also a way for organizations to show their commitment to each employee as a person.

Again, lululemon stands out here. The company's willingness to stay connected to, and support, former employees has created a nexus of entrepreneurial companies in Vancouver, spanning multiple industries including apparel, food services, and fitness. Many employees who depart to pursue dreams of opening a studio or a gym later become "ambassadors," their pictures proudly displayed in local lululemon stores to showcase their new ventures. This demonstrates to current employees how deeply invested the company is in the ongoing success of those who came before them—whether or not that success is within the confines of the company.

One Size Fits One

Brain science reveals that there are more synaptic connections in each human brain than there are stars in 5,000 Milky Ways, resulting in endless variations in how we all think and feel. It shouldn't be surprising, therefore, that people in the same job love and do their work very differently. An organization dedicated to love builds its people practices around that fact. (See the sidebar "Different Ways to Love the Same Job.") To help people pinpoint their particular pattern of loves and loathings and channel them into contribution, an organization must empower teams and team leaders to make the most of each employee's uniqueness.

Avoid tools that standardize

Competency models, feedback tools, and rigid career paths, which have become the norm at most large companies today, replace employees' personal loves with cookie-cutter actions or behaviors. At Love + Work organizations, in contrast, each role is defined by a very few measured outcomes rather than by a competency model. Thus hotel general managers are measured according to occupancy

Different Ways to Love the Same Job

AS PART OF ITS ONGOING STUDY OF EXCELLENCE AT WORK, ADPRI does primary qualitative research involving top performers in a variety of roles. Here, for example, are the words of three excellent hotel general managers describing what they love about their job:

- "It almost sounds strange, I know, but I actually love it when an angry guest marches up to the front desk. I find my brain works faster, my adrenaline pumping; it feels amazing, like I'm on edge, but loving it. Guess I have a superhero complex, right?"

- "My best moments are trying to figure out how to get my team to jell. It's hard because you've got all these different personalities, different schedules, different roles, and somehow I've got to arrange it all so that you've got the right people doing the right things at the right time. Of course, I never get it quite right, but I'm so into it."

- "People say I'm never satisfied, but I don't think of it like that. I love taking something that's working and then figuring out newer and better ways of doing things. I get bored so quickly. So if it's new, never been done before, first time, I'm right there. I can't tell you how many times we've redone our team awards or our guest appreciation programs. I'll never stop."

levels and guest satisfaction ratings. Nurses are held accountable for patient outcomes and patient satisfaction scores. Salespeople are measured by sales volume and client growth. And so on. When outcomes are carefully identified and calibrated, employees can pinpoint the activities they love and be helped to find their own path toward those outcomes. The explosive growth of coaching-as-a-service companies such as BetterUp is but one sign that companies are moving away from standardization and toward offering individual guidance to employees at all levels.

These organizations also avoid feedback tools, which by definition measure each person against a standardized list of skills or competencies. I've previously explained in this magazine why feedback is pernicious ("The Feedback Fallacy," HBR, March–April 2019). In short: People's feedback is inevitably colored by their own loves (and loathings) and offers precious little to help other employees discover and contribute theirs. Aside from input about facts or required steps, feedback generally consists of one person—however well-intentioned—smothering another.

Organizing around love of the work means that no career paths are defined by the skills or competencies required at each level—indeed, no research that I know of in any refereed journal proves that the best practitioners in a given role all have the same skills and competencies. Competency models are an abstraction that denies the real-world truth that people in the same role find love in very different activities and aspects of it—and, therefore, they thrive and excel in the role using quite different methods. Careers will increasingly be designed according to an employee's own interests and skills. AI-based software offerings such as Gloat, Fuel50, and Flux are the leaders in a growing pack of platforms that build career paths in this way.

Focus on teams

To avoid standardization, companies must organize around teams.

In 2019, as my ADPRI colleagues and I were analyzing the data from our global study of the world's workers, we discovered just how important teams are to employees. Workers who reported that they felt part of a team were not only 2.7 times as likely as others to be fully engaged, but also three times as likely to be highly resilient and twice as likely to report a strong sense of belonging to their organization.

That's because teams make a home for idiosyncrasy. In a team, each person's unique loves and loathings can be combined with those of others to create something greater than any one person could achieve alone. Humans have long known this. In fact, the oldest human art ever discovered is a 45,000-year-old painting on a cave wall on the island of Sulawesi that depicts a small group of hunters, each drawn with a different animal characteristic thought to denote the particular contribution of each team member: the trunk of an elephant to show the strength of one, the tail of a crocodile to symbolize the cunning of another. "There is no 'I' in 'team'" misses the fundamental point of a team, which is precisely to capitalize on the contribution of each unique 'I.' If you're on a team and your manager and teammates see and know your loves, they can find ways to help you do work that you love better than a blind organization ever could.

But today most organizations are *not* built around teams. Although plenty of teamwork is happening, leaders can't see it or take advantage of it. Just look at most existing human-capital-management software. It displays individuals and who they report to, but not which teams they're on.

An organization with a focus on teams institutes formal team-joining programs in which people learn why they were picked for their assignments. This introduction includes detailed descriptions of the skills and talents they bring to their teams and what they can rely on or turn to each teammate for. Patagonia takes its team building out of headquarters with hiking trips to the nearby Santa Ynez mountains or campfires on the beach in Ventura to help team members see one another as whole, unique people. There they might learn that one member loves working under pressure, another is most creative from 6 a.m. to noon, and another must do a three-mile run around the neighborhood every morning or lose motivation. As more and more people work remotely, companies will have to be even more intentional about making joining a team a critical part of onboarding. I expect that we'll see lots of software applications emerging to fill this space.

But the most important part of being on a team is developing trust with the individuals who constitute it.

In Trust We Grow

The data supports a strong link between trust and all the good outcomes that love at work produces. When ADPRI asked its 50,000 global survey participants if they trusted their teammates, their team leader, and their senior leaders, those who strongly agreed that they trusted people in two of the three categories were three times as likely as others to be fully engaged and highly resilient. Those who strongly agreed that they trusted all three were 15 times as likely to be fully engaged and 42 times as likely to be highly resilient.

That's because trust drives the ability of employees to discover and do what they love. In a study of housekeepers at Disney World, I found that many loved their job specifically because they could be creative about how to do it. One rearranged children's stuffed animals into different scenes each day, for example. Another lay down on the bed to check the room from that angle because she knew that would be the first thing a guest did after a long day in the park. The trust given the housekeepers to exercise their autonomy—despite official rules to the contrary—was what made them love their jobs, and that love allowed them to excel in ways that no checklist of tasks could possibly do.

To deliberately engender trust in your organization, you'll need to end certain rituals and start others.

Discard rituals that erode trust

Goals cascaded down from above, performance ratings, and 360-degree surveys—mechanisms that we tend to think of as increasing alignment and boosting performance—too often signal that the organization doesn't trust its people. Goals imposed from above are artificial and disconnect employees from thinking through what they love and how they can contribute it. In contrast, a Love + Work organization trusts people to set their own goals, which are discussed and adjusted as necessary during the course of the year.

I've previously written in *Harvard Business Review* ("Reinventing Performance Management," HBR, April 2015) about why performance ratings are unreliable. No one trusts them—even the people getting the highest ratings. With everyone reduced to a number, the organization can't see the whole person. Similarly, everyone suspects, rightly, that 360-degree surveys generate unreliable data that in no way reveals who a particular employee is. These mechanisms convey to employees that they are monitored but without any real trust that they know what it takes to do their jobs.

Instead, pay attention

Love + Work organizations build trust by actually paying attention to employees through their team leaders. This requires empowering those leaders and reducing their span of responsibility so that frequent, individualized attention is possible.

Organizations that build trust view a once-a-week check-in between employees and team leaders as the core human ritual at work. During this chat the team leader will not be checking up on or appraising the person or giving feedback. Instead the leader will be talking about the short-term past and future, asking, "What did you love about last week?" "What did you loathe?" "What are your priorities this coming week?" "How can I best help?"

Asking those four questions every week for an entire year will ensure that employees build trust with their team leaders. It doesn't appear to matter whether the check-in happens in person, on the phone, by email, or in an app. What matters is simply that it happens. During a check-in both people can talk about the specifics of the work the employee is doing, the challenges that might be arising, and what the team leader can do to help. Each sharing of a challenge and each small action to provide support help build trust between them. But not only that: Naming the specific activities they loved the previous week keeps employees' loves front and center, tied tightly to the real work that needs to get done.

Many organizations have already instituted the check-in as a core ritual. Cisco alone averages more than 3 million check-ins a year. It is not a cure-all, of course: Some team leaders merely go through the motions, and some employees take a long time to feel that the organization genuinely cares about who they are and what they love. But the data from millions of check-ins is compelling. Team leaders who check in every week drive their team members' engagement scores up by 77% and their team members' voluntary turnover in the following six months down by 67%.

To make this ritual possible, Love + Work organizations eschew departments or functions so large that the span of control makes it impossible for a team leader to check in with each team member. A ratio of one leader to 70 members might make financial sense on a balance sheet, but it makes little sense for people trying to build trust.

Our leaders publicly announce that they want us to return to work, but for many of us, the current tensions regarding work all stem from our questioning whether we even want to go back to an earlier way of doing things. "Normal" led us into a workplace ecosystem that seemed designed to exploit us and stress us and reduce our agency. Normal made us unhealthy. If organizations dismiss employees' reticence or just hope that it will pass by, they will forever struggle to attract the best people and wonder why they have such trouble keeping the ones they do attract.

In contrast, the smartest organizations will recognize that if they can redesign work with love at its core, they will be able to make new and more-genuine commitments to their workers and over time will become magnets for talent. They will truly deserve the best people.

Originally published in May–June 2022. Reprint R2203C

About the Contributors

SCOTT D. ANTHONY is a clinical professor at Dartmouth College's Tuck School of Business, a senior partner at Innosight, and the lead author of *Eat, Sleep, Innovate* and *Dual Transformation* (both Harvard Business Review Press, 2020 and 2017, respectively).

MARCUS BUCKINGHAM is the head of people and performance research at the ADP Research Institute, the author of *Love and Work*, and a coauthor of *Nine Lies About Work* (both Harvard Business Review Press, 2022 and 2019, respectively).

J. YO-JUD CHENG is an assistant professor of business administration in the Strategy, Ethics and Entrepreneurship area at the University of Virginia's Darden School of Business.

PAUL COBBAN is the former chief data and transformation officer at DBS Bank, based in Singapore, and a coauthor of *Eat, Sleep, Innovate* (Harvard Business Review Press, 2020).

ROB CROSS is the Edward A. Madden Professor of Global Leadership at Babson College, founder of the Connected Commons, and the author of *Beyond Collaboration Overload* (Harvard Business Review Press, 2021).

ROBIN J. ELY is the Diane Doerge Wilson Professor of Business Administration at Harvard Business School and the faculty chair of the HBS Gender Initiative.

DANIEL GOLEMAN, best known for his writing on emotional intelligence, is the codirector of the Consortium for Research on Emotional Intelligence in Organizations at Rutgers University. His latest compilation is Building Blocks of Emotional Intelligence, a 12-primer series on each of the emotional intelligence competencies, and he offers training on the competencies through an online learning platform, Emotional Intelligence Training Courses. His other books include *Primal Leadership* and *Altered Traits*.

BORIS GROYSBERG is the Richard P. Chapman Professor of Business Administration in the Organizational Behavior unit at Harvard Business School.

JOHN S. HAMMOND was a consultant on decision-making, a former professor at Harvard Business School, and a coauthor of *Smart Choices* (Harvard Business School Press, 1998).

RALPH L. KEENEY is a professor emeritus at Duke University's Fuqua School of Business and a coauthor of *Smart Choices* (Harvard Business School Press, 1998).

JOHN P. KOTTER is a bestselling author, an award-winning business and management thought leader, a business entrepreneur, and the Konosuke Matsushita Professor of Leadership, Emeritus, at Harvard Business School. His ideas, books, and company, Kotter, help people lead organizations in an era of increasingly rapid change. He is a coauthor of the book *Change*, which details how leaders can leverage challenges and opportunities to make sustainable workplace changes in a rapidly accelerating world.

JEREMIAH LEE leads innovation for advisory services at Spencer Stuart. He and Jesse Price are cofounders of two culture-related businesses.

PAUL LEINWAND is the global managing director for capabilities-driven strategy and growth at Strategy&, PwC's strategy consulting business. He is a principal with PwC U.S., an adjunct professor of strategy at Northwestern University's Kellogg School of Management, and a coauthor of several books, including *Beyond Digital* and *Strategy That Works* (both Harvard Business Review Press, 2022 and 2016, respectively).

MAHADEVA MATT MANI is a principal with PwC U.S. He leads the transformation platform for PwC and for its strategy consulting business, Strategy&, advising executives on business-model transformations, operational value creation, and productivity programs. He is a coauthor of *Beyond Digital* (Harvard Business Review Press, 2022).

MICHAEL C. MANKINS is a leader in Bain's organization and strategy practices and a partner in Austin, Texas. He is a coauthor of *Time, Talent, Energy* (Harvard Business Review Press, 2017).

RITA GUNTHER McGRATH is a professor at Columbia Business School and a globally recognized expert on strategy in uncertain and volatile environments. She is the author of *The End of Competitive Advantage* and *Seeing Around Corners*.

RAHUL NAIR is a manager at Innosight.

NATALIE PAINCHAUD is an associate partner at Innosight and a coauthor of *Eat, Sleep, Innovate* (Harvard Business Review Press, 2020).

JESSE PRICE is a leader in organizational culture services at Spencer Stuart. He and Jeremiah Lee are cofounders of two culture-related businesses.

HOWARD RAIFFA was the Frank Plumpton Ramsey Professor of Managerial Economics, Emeritus, at Harvard Business School and a coauthor of *Smart Choices* (Harvard Business School Press, 1998).

BLAIR SHEPPARD is the global leader of strategy and leadership for the PwC network. He directs the team that is responsible for articulating PwC's global strategy across 156 countries and developing current and next-generation PwC leaders. He is also a professor emeritus and dean emeritus of Duke University's Fuqua School of Business and the author of *Ten Years to Midnight*.

DAVID A. THOMAS is the president of Morehouse College. He is also the H. Naylor Fitzhugh Professor Emeritus at Harvard Business School and the former dean of Georgetown University's McDonough School of Business.

ROBERT THOMAS is a leadership and teams consultant. He was previously a managing director at the Accenture Institute for High Performance. He is the author of eight books on leadership and organizational change, including *Crucibles of Leadership*, *Geeks and Geezers* (with Warren Bennis), and *Driving Results Through Social Networks* (with Rob Cross).

Index

[Handwritten notes:]

newsletter?

- Outcomes review
- questions
  - how do admins collaborate across depts / service lines
  - how do pts come to MTC?
  - new space ~ such an integrated practice
- opportunities
  - 3-site+ health system
  - living donation!
  - allocation-related
  - NRP / perfusion
  - DCD
  - regenerative medicine
  - outpatient: 5-year outcomes
  - pt. decision tools

VISION

* weight-loss protocol

SRTR